The **Photographing Tourist**

A Storyteller's Guide to Travel and Photography

by David Noyes

© 2015 David Noyes. All rights reserved.

No part of this publication may be reproduced, stored in a retrieval system, or transmitted in any form or by any means, electronic, mechanical, photocopying, recording, or otherwise, without the prior written permission of the publisher.

For permission requests, contact the publisher.
www.noyestravels.com

Library of Congress Control Number: 2015910124

ISBN: 978-0-9965239-0-5

Published by D.F. Noyes Studios, Buffalo, New York

Design by Linda Prinzi, Goulah Design Group, Inc.

Printed in the United States of America

Acknowledgments

Publishing this book was most certainly a team effort. Many people over many years contributed to the generation of the stories and photographs, and many others helped shape its look and presentation. Most of the written travel narratives began as magazine articles that were printed in periodicals all over the world. My first thank you must go out to the editors that have published my work and the many tour operators, travel companies, and marketing organizations that hosted me or guided me on my adventures.

There are also several individuals who helped this book go from a distant possibility to a reality. Fellow travel journalists Kristen Gill and Marlene Goldman did edits of the original manuscript and second draft respectively, and graphic designer Jennifer Bernthal contributed the initial look and feel to my vision while it was still in its infancy.

Traveling to far away places can also be hard on those left behind. My mother, Nancy; sister, Debby Brown; and my wife, Barbara, have spent countless hours following my itineraries and worrying about me in some remote and distant land. But they have always encouraged me to follow my passion to see the world and share my stories—well maybe not my mom so much. She would prefer me to stay at home.

Lastly, I would like to recognize two very special people who died during the creation of this book. Peter Muigai Muruthi was a safari guide in Kenya, but he was also a warm and generous man who helped educate children in need. I shared a lot of wonderful moments with Muigai, and he was the inspiration for my charity *Innocent Eyes Project*, which follows his lead to help educate some of the world's poorest children. Rest in peace, *rafiki*. And then there is my father, Frank. Dad never shared my desire to travel and explore the world, but he is the reason that I have the courage to follow my dreams. There are no words to describe how much he is missed.

Contents

iii	**Acknowledgments**
ix	**Preface**
xi	**Introduction**
xi	Traveling with Innocent Eyes

Chapter 1
1 Going Beyond the Snapshot
- 2   The Tourist Trap
- 2   Birth of the Snapshot
- 4   Traveling as a Photographer
- 6   Writing with Light
- 9   Finding Your Zone

Chapter 2
21 Local Lifestyles
- 22   People to People
- 23   Beware of the Cute Kid with a Baby Lamb
- 24   Indigenous Tourism
- 25   Pokot Encounter
- 27   A Wild Ride

Chapter 3
53 Where People Gather
- 54   A Gift from Innocent Eyes
- 54   Scenes of Daily Life
- 56   Humor and Irony
- 58   Environmental Portrait
- 59   A World at Work
- 61   A Compelling Face
- 63   Human Connections

Chapter 4
75 Spiritual Worlds and Sacred Places
- 76   Cultural Etiquette
- 77   Houses of Worship
- 79   Worshipers, Offerings, and Rituals
- 80   Monks and Nuns
- 83   Symbols and Sacred Objects

OPPOSITE PAGE: Lake Atitlán, Guatamala

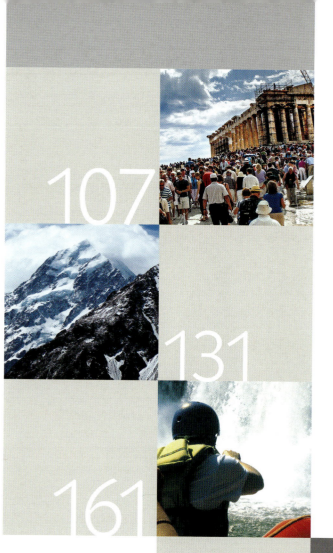

Chapter 5
107 Landmarks and Famous Places
- 108 The Tourist Challenge
- 109 Port of Call
- 110 More to the Story
- 113 This Place is Ruined
- 117 Photographing the Tourists' Experience

Chapter 6
131 Nature's Spectacle
- 132 Seeing the Light
- 134 Landscapes and Scenics
- 136 Golden Hour
- 137 Embracing White
- 139 Local Wildlife

Chapter 7
161 The Adventure Begins
- 162 Getting There
- 163 A Watery World
- 165 Peeking Below the Waves
- 167 Going to Extremes

Chapter 8
183 Forces of Change

207 Index

Technical Shorts
- 3 Composition
- 5 Bullseye Effect
- 5 Rule of Thirds
- 7 Sidelight and Backlight
- 22 Angle of View
- 26 Point of View
- 57 Elements of Design
- 60 Principles of Design
- 78 Artificial Light
- 81 Fill Flash
- 111 Controlling Focus
- 111 Depth of Field
- 114 The Blind Shot
- 135 Using Lines
- 136 Exposure
- 138 A Filtered Effect
- 163 A Matter of Perspective
- 166 Vanishing Point

Final Word
203 Through Innocent Eyes

INNOCENT EYES PROJECT.ORG

FIELD NOTES

- 10 — Connect Before You Click — **1** Kenya
- 30 — A Hill Tribe Spectacle — **2** Thailand
- 64 — Alone Time in Kolkata — **3** India
- 84 — Sunrise Over Bagan — **4** Myanmar
- 86 — A Holy City in a Holy Land — **5** Israel
- 118 — Awakening the Dragon — **6** China
- 120 — The Lost City of the Inca — **7** Peru
- 142 — Europe's Coolest Little Hot Spot — **8** Iceland
- 170 — Alaska Cruise Adventure — **9** United States
- 172 — Midnight Accent — **10** Tanzania

features

- 12 — The Rite of Passage
- 34 — China's New Silk Road
- 44 — Nepal Through Innocent Eyes
- 66 — Gypsies, Gods, and Dromedaries
- 88 — The Sacred City of Shiva
- 98 — The Lure of Tibet
- 122 — Romantic Expectations
- 144 — The Greatest Show on Earth
- 152 — Greenland's Icy Lure
- 174 — The Everest Highway
- 184 — The Enchanted Isles
- 194 — Naked by Choice

The Photographing Tourist

Preface

OPPOSITE PAGE LEFT TO RIGHT: Lhasa, Tibet; Chichen Itza, Mexico
BELOW LEFT TO RIGHT: Narsaq, Greenland; Jerusalem, Israel

As a photographer and travel writer, I have been fortunate to visit some of the world's great places and witness both the beauty and tragedy of the human condition. This book represents over a decade of my work as a travel journalist and was written for travelers who want to use their camera to explore a destination, culture, environment, or landscape in more depth than a simple travel snapshot can reveal. It is intended to educate and inform while also taking you on a journey to remote corners of the world.

The chapters explore different photographic subjects that a tourist photographer will encounter, from portraits and local life to landmarks and landscapes. Each chapter begins with advice, suggestions, and illustrations to help you feel more confident as a travel photographer, followed by anecdotes and stories from my travel adventures. Some are fun and whimsical; others are intricate stories about complex places, but they all attempt to bring the travel experience to life by sharing a series of travel images with the narrative story they illustrate.

Through a blend of stories, tips, and techniques, these pages will help you to think like a travel photographer and hopefully inspire you to go beyond simply collecting pictures of world sites you visit and to investigate a destination as part of the human condition. It was written to be a timeless book that is as much about the experience of traveling as a photographer as it is the techniques of travel photography. Above all, I hope this book helps you to truly cherish your chance encounters as you photograph the world.

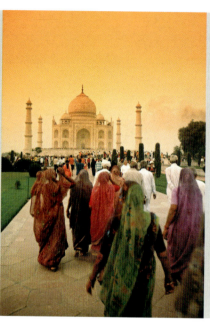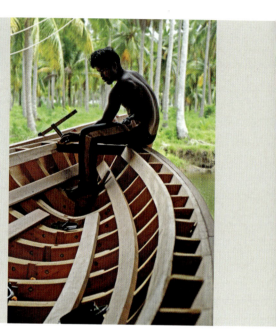

OPPOSITE PAGE LEFT TO RIGHT: Phang Nga, Thailand; Agra, India; Phang Nga Bay, Thailand; Khao Lak, Thailand
BELOW LEFT TO RIGHT: Beijing, China; Rift Valley, Kenya

Introduction

Find authenticity along the edges of your adventures.

Traveling with Innocent Eyes

Limuru is a bustling small town with a lively local market and many small shops that service thousands of people from the surrounding area. We stopped briefly to buy beans to fill the bags I brought as camera supports for shooting wildlife in the game parks on my first trip to Kenya. The stop also gave me an opportunity to photograph the largely Kikuyu population living just north of Nairobi. The crowds of mostly men and boys were aggressive as they noticed my camera. We were instantly confronted by swarms of people as we walked away from the truck. Many of the boys were visibly stoned from sniffing glue, and the curiosity of strangers in town created a palpable excitement. I learned quickly that candid shots in towns and villages would be virtually impossible. Each individual portrait or storefront photograph often required a lengthy process of negotiation to fix an appropriate fee.

Each day, I struggled to control my anxiety. Being constantly surrounded by dozens of people in an unfamiliar country made it difficult to concentrate on taking pictures. Shooting in towns and villages was far too intense and intimidating to even consider light, subject, and composition. Working there was about instinct

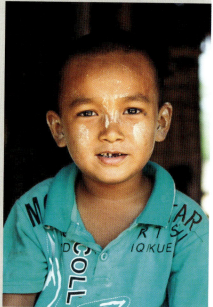

OPPOSITE PAGE TOP LEFT TO RIGHT: Roseau, Dominica; Pushkar, India; Cuzco, Peru; Swakopmund, Namibia
OPPOSITE PAGE BOTTOM LEFT TO RIGHT: Cuzco, Peru; Roseau, Dominica; Taxkorgan, China; Bagan, Myanmar

and reaction. I had to make fast decisions and assimilate a lot of information about the environment, not to mention trying to remember what film I had loaded, checking the ISO rating and exposure, and setting the shutter speed and f/stop while also interacting with my negotiators, translators, aggressive hawkers, and reluctant models. I was way outside of my comfort zone.

Before arriving in Kenya, I had several preconceived and rational ideas about what I wished to accomplish. I was going to shoot what I saw, forgetting the stereotypical images of African poverty, and explore the reality of life as a detached and objective witness. I went to Africa to challenge my understanding of the world and to challenge myself as a professional photographer. I went to Africa with a plan!

It didn't take long to realize that my skills as a corporate and advertising photographer didn't apply in East Africa. All of my plans and expectations evaporated as soon as our Range Rover came to a stop. I found working in the unpredictable and often overwhelming situations to be the most challenging and rewarding experience of my life. It required me to find the courage to engage the unfamiliar and let go of my sense of control. It taught me to travel with innocent eyes, without preconception or prejudice, and to let the experience simply unfold in front of me. I also learned that it is impossible to travel into the world's poorest communities and not be moved by courageous people who confront issues of survival that most of us simply take for granted.

As the title of this book suggests, my travel experiences have almost always been on an organized tour or cruise, with a planned itinerary, accompanied by a group of strangers. They have been trips that I designed and led, trips I have escorted for tour operators, press trips I was invited to join, conference excursions, or custom itineraries with my wife on a holiday adventure. In essence, I have experienced the world and enjoyed success in travel journalism as a professional "tourist."

Don't get me wrong, an organized tour can be a wonderful experience. It is an opportunity to meet new people and make new friends. You travel with an escort, a guide, and a translator. All the details are preplanned and prearranged. You just need to relax and go along with the flow. But the experience can be pretty insulating and superficial. It is virtually impossible to obtain a deep understanding of a people or a place on an organized tourist trip. That doesn't mean that you can't produce great photography on a tour; it just means you need to work faster and find authenticity along the edges of your adventures.

Many of my travel images depict classic attractions or contrived events and situations packaged and presented for tourist consumption. The challenge is to think differently and make the most of the thirty minutes, hour, or two hours before moving on to the next location. I have actually grown to enjoy the challenge of a deadline, the uncertainty of my circumstances, and the lack of control.

Over the years, I found that I was collecting much more than a portfolio of travel images; I was collecting stories. Stories about the chance encounters I was having along the way and stories about how these experiences have changed my understanding of the world. A photograph simply can't explain the warmth I felt in my soul from the toothless smile of a beautiful Tibetan woman or truly describe how a spectacular mountain landscape left me breathless. My photographs had become the catalyst for storytelling and my stories added depth and meaning to my images. It is these unexpected and unplanned moments on tour when you too will create a lifetime of travel memories.

OPPOSITE PAGE: Maho Beach, Saint Martin

Chapter 1
Going Beyond the Snapshot

tour·ist *noun* \ˈtu̇r-ist\
: a person who travels to a place for pleasure

Venturing into an unfamiliar place can be a frightening and intimidating experience, even for a seasoned traveler. Today, you can literally get on a plane and physically travel thousands of miles in a matter of hours and in some remote corners of the world be culturally transported thousands of years back in time. But familiarizing yourself with transportation options, culture, local customs, language, and the risks of independent travel can make even the preparation for a trip abroad nerve racking. The option most people choose is the guided or escorted tour—the "tour" in tourist.

What we call tourism developed in the late nineteenth century as people with more leisure time started to spread the word that something was "worth seeing." The purpose of travel, of course, is to explore and experience; to see the world for ourselves. In the past few years, affordable group tours have been developed for nearly every interest: culinary tours, cultural tours, historical tours, backpacking, kayaking, biking, volunteering tours, and spiritual tours are just a few. You name it and you can share your experience with people with common interests on a packed itinerary loaded with activities.

OPPOSITE PAGE: Cancun, Mexico

The Tourist Trap

The words *tourism* and *tourist* are often used pejoratively to suggest a shallow interest in cultures and destinations. This is the stereotypical vision of a camera-laden foreigner carrying a map or guidebook, snapping pictures of popular attractions. An often-quoted insight by early twentieth century English novelist and essayist Gilbert K. Chesterton puts the tourist versus traveler debate like this: "The traveler sees what he sees; the tourist sees what he has come to see."

Yes, being a tourist with a packed itinerary means that your travel experience will be more superficial, and you will probably keep to the beaten path more than someone who is spending months exploring indigenous cultures in Southeast Asia or roaming independently across Europe living within local communities. Simply put, it is virtually impossible to be immersive on a packaged vacation or holiday abroad, no matter what your intent.

For a photographer, traveling as a part of an organized tour also presents many challenges. Most significant is the constraint of an itinerary. By definition, an itinerary means that you will be at this place, at this time, for this long, and you will most likely never be back. You might travel halfway around the world to one of the world's great wonders and be instructed by your escort to "meet back at the bus in thirty minutes." Or trek for weeks only to find the mountaintop of your muse shrouded in clouds.

As a photographer on a tour, you get what you get: blue sky, white sky, rain, crowds, no crowds, overhead sun, no sun, empty markets, wrong time of day, wrong time of year. You get the point. You have no control over the circumstances of your shoot. Whatever happens… happens. This is why most tourists are usually disappointed when they compare their snapshots with local postcards shot by a professional under perfect conditions.

Birth of the Snapshot

The only thing necessary to turn a tourist into a photographer is a camera. In fact, the two go hand in hand. It would seem unnatural to travel for leisure and not carry a camera to record your experiences as visual souvenirs.

Throughout most of its history, beginning in 1839, photography of far away places has been produced by professionals and consumed by aspiring travelers. Throughout the nineteenth century, the process of photography was scientific and technical. Cameras were cumbersome and the chemistry to process the latent image was potentially dangerous to the practitioner. But as photographs became cheap and mass produced, they made the world both visible and desirable to a leisure class with the means to travel. Yet it wasn't until the late 1880s that tourists themselves had the ability to capture their own photographic moments.

In 1888, George Eastman launched the first user-friendly roll film camera. The camera sold for twenty-five dollars with enough film for one hundred photographs. After the film was exposed, the entire camera was sent back to the Eastman Dry Plate and Film Company for processing and printing. Marketed with the slogan

It wasn't until the late 1880s that tourists themselves had the ability to capture their own photographic moments.

Composition

Before you can begin to compose a photograph, you need to be aware of what is going on around you and what is going on inside the frame. From an early age we have learned how to read visual cues and we respond to these bits of language very quickly. Where you place subjects in an image changes their relative weight. Big areas of brightness or strong shadows, colors, and simple things like eye contact also contribute to the visual hierarchy that results in an image that has symmetry and balance.

Unlike a painter who chooses where to place each element in a picture, travel photographers can only frame what they find. It is not just what you shoot that makes an impactful photograph, it is equally important how you shoot it. The arrangement of elements in the frame is what we call composition, and a bad composition can make even a great subject a mediocre photograph.

As you travel, you will encounter a wide range of subjects and scenes. What works for one photograph might not work for another. As you become familiar with aspects of good composition, you will understand how simple choices about focal length and angle of view will affect how your photographs communicate and are perceived by viewers. Being able to recognize and control the elements in a photograph is the difference between a snapshot of the scene and a photograph seen through the trained eye of an artist.

OPPOSITE PAGE CLOCKWISE: **Isla Chira, Costa Rica; Hotan, China; Beijing, China**

"You Press the Button, We Do the Rest," the Kodak camera turned the once difficult, physically dangerous profession of photography into a popular hobby. The snapshot was born.

From that point on, photography and tourism have been forever linked. Kodak made photography accessible to millions of amateurs with no technical skill, training, or aesthetic credentials. Today everybody is a photographer, everywhere, all the time. "Snap…look…delete" has become its own amusing tourist performance. The ability to constantly check the results on our LCD (liquid-crystal display) has become so ubiquitous that it has even inspired its own verb, "chimping." Every day millions of images are taken and uploaded to computer networks in a global phenomenon. The latest tourist snapshot trend, the "selfie," is instantly transported around the world, announcing to friends, family, and followers "Look where I am."

For more serious tourist photographers, digital photography is a true blessing. Not only can we see our exposure, focus, lighting, and composition at a glance, we can use the little images in the back of the camera to interact with the subjects of our attention. Nothing breaks the ice with strangers better than showing them the results of their portrait. By freeing the photographer from the cost of film, the digital revolution has opened the opportunity for tourist photographers to explore their artistic aspirations by being more creative and adventurous. If it doesn't work, just push "delete."

Traveling as a Photographer

The snapshot (selfie notwithstanding) is most often considered to be a simple view of a person or landscape where the subject is placed in the center of the frame, shot from eye level, with no thought to composition, and often with the sun directly behind the photographer. It has come to be defined as a poorly composed and spontaneously shot image without any artistic or journalistic intent. But more than the aesthetic of the snapshot, the snapshot is a product of the mind, not the camera. It represents an emotionally detached record of an event with little or no effort to compose a more interesting image. If you train your eye to really see what you are looking at, great travel images can be taken with any device that can capture an image.

Unlike other forms of journalism where "truth" is paramount and the content supersedes the presentation, much of the travel

Bullseye Effect

When you place the main subject smack-dab in the center of the frame, it will dominate the photograph and you miss the opportunity to create interplay with secondary details. If you are going to create a bullseye effect in the center of the frame to concentrate attention on the main subject, there must be other dynamics to drive the story and generate interest. Each part of the image needs to contribute to the overall composition.

Rule of Thirds

Simply stated, the Rule of Thirds is a classic compositional guideline suggesting that if you divide an image into three equal parts, both up-and-down and side-to-side, elements placed near or at the intersection of those lines will have the most impact. The rule forces the main subject of the image off-center, helping to create a more interesting composition.

This technique works well with almost any subject, but you don't need to be obsessive about the rule, just start taking the time to move the main object of your photograph slightly off center. This works particularly well when the subject is easily identifiable and surrounded by a simple background, like a portrait. The visual weight of the object is usually balanced by the vast negative space, but if not, look for other satellite elements including line, color, or contrast to find visual balance.

RIGHT: Namib Desert, Namibia
OPPOSITE PAGE: Kashgar, China

photography we respond to and wish to emulate is unapologetically decorative. The tourist photographer seeks to photograph the beautiful, the exotic, the unfamiliar, the historic, and the icons of travel. But the photograph will need other qualities to transcend the merely picturesque, captivate the viewer, and tell a story.

To make your photographs more interesting, more powerful, and more artistic, you are forced to engage, to see what others might overlook, and to notice the small things that capture the character of a place. If you use your camera with the intention of exploring a destination, culture, environment, or landscape, it will change your travel experience, change the way you interact with people, and ultimately change the quality and meaning of your images.

As you become immersed in the environment, the act of photographing becomes the experience. Your camera work isn't just the means to an end (producing photographs), it is an end in itself. You are no longer simply sightseeing or passively looking, you are actively engaged in creating your own interactive travel memories, potentially more valuable than any of the resulting images. The goal is to return home not just with a collection of photographs, but to have learned something about yourself and the subjects of your photographs by letting each culture, person, and place you visit impact you along the way.

Writing with Light

We live in a world filled with images. From newspapers, books, and magazines to television screens and computer monitors, we are bombarded daily with pictorial representations of the world. As children, even before we begin to read and write, we begin to absorb visual data and learn to comprehend the representational meaning through experience. Outside of an art class or two, most of us were not taught how to make pictures. In school we were taught how to read stories, not how to read images.

We all recognize the content of most photographs as something familiar: a tree, a person, a building, a landscape, etc. These common visual stimuli are also linked to human emotions that affect our interpretation of a photograph. We respond to images instinc-

Sidelight and Backlight

The old rule of thumb for successful photography is to keep the sun at your back and avoid harsh shadows. It is a rule of thumb because following it will produce well-exposed, evenly lit photographs. It is also the most predictable and least creative use of light. Since all the shadows of a front-lit scene are falling behind the subject and away from the camera, it is considered a "flat" light that lacks any sense of depth. Strong shadows and texture created by a sidelight are usually more interesting and dramatic. Since the light is scraping across the object, it creates large and small shadows that exaggerate surface textures, define depth, and enhance the tactile qualities of a subject.

The low sidelight created near sunset is perfect for landscapes like deserts and beaches, giving them a three-dimensional quality. A strong sidelight in a portrait can create drama and help bring out emotion, while a diffused sidelight from a window or a slight overcast will contour delicate facial features with soft shadows. Sidelights also offer the best opportunity to design with shadows by using the well-defined dark areas in the composition.

Backlight, by definition, means that you are shooting into a light source. It is the trickiest use of light but can produce theatrical and dramatic effects. The stronger the light source, the greater the backlight effect will be. Soft backlights for portraits will create a rim light that separates the subject from the background without their face being lost in shadow. A powerful backlight is needed to create silhouettes, and shadows coming directly toward the camera will exaggerate depth and distance.

tively. When we look at picture of a beautiful little girl, a charging elephant, or a spectacular sunset on a tropical beach, we have a visceral reaction. There is no delay in our comprehension. We understand.

Without light there is no photography. We often take for granted the daily effects of light and how subtle changes in its abundance, direction, and quality actually contribute to our happiness and how we view the world. Trained photographers are both students and careful observers of light. Light has direction that can reveal texture, depth, dimension, shape, and volume. Light bounces and reflects, it is hard and soft, it is a friend and it is a nemesis.

All light has direction. In the natural world, light originates from a point source 92,960,000 miles (149,600,000 km) away from Earth, which we call the sun. It is very predictable. It rises in the east and sets in the west, and in between it moves from horizon to horizon at a predictable rate of speed.

In travel photography the most common light source is daylight. From the first glow of a rising sun to the last rays of sunset, the color and quality of daylight is constantly changing. A scene illuminated by the beautiful predawn wash of pink and blue will transform within hours as shadows shorten and intensify and the sun brightens to its fullest strength. As the day unfolds, texture is created and lost, complex landscapes are exposed and then hidden, and enchanting details are discovered or concealed as the earth rotates and revolves.

Understanding how light works and how to use it effectively is one of the surest ways to improve your photography. There is no "good" or "bad" light. Different natural light effects lend themselves to different photographs. Light is a tool to communicate mood and atmosphere. You can train yourself to recognize the effects of light by observing it in your everyday life. Open your eyes to how light moves across the landscape at varying heights and intensities and how it is affected by different atmospheric conditions. Watch as shadows move when you move. Notice how light streams through a window or doorway, creating pools of light and shadow.

Finding Your Zone

Creating interesting and memorable photographs takes time: time to observe what is going on around you, time to see the effects of light on the scene, and time to sense the rhythm of a place. For a tourist photographer with limited time to make decisions, these observations need to happen quickly. Like any skill, being able to focus intensely on the task at hand comes with training. Take a few minutes to simply watch, and let your natural excitement turn into a focused concentration.

For me, when the bus, truck, or van doors open, it is "game time." The initial shot of adrenaline as I enter a crowded street market or tribal village kicks me into a hyperalert state. As the initial kick-start begins to fade, I enter a more relaxed state where my visual senses are sharpened, and movement, shape, color, and contrast catch my eye as I scan the scene in front of me. Photographs begin to frame themselves. The camera becomes an extension of my eyes. Athletes call that state "being in the zone."

Every activity has an optimal state of adrenaline-fueled stimulation. You need to develop the same psychological skills used by elite athletes to control the effects of stimulation and maintain control of your attention. If you are so overwhelmed with a situation that you can't concentrate, you certainly won't be able frame the world into interesting photographs. Likewise, if you are not in your zone because you are bored or distracted, you won't be able to "see" photographs in the scene unfolding in front of you.

If you lose your focus or concentration, the first thing you need to do is realize that you are no longer in your zone and choose a strategy to get back in it. Taking pictures while traveling is very different than traveling as a photographer. If you are bored, energize yourself by approaching a stranger for a conversation or portrait. If you are excited, calm down by stepping aside for a few minutes to just watch and relax.

When I pick up the camera, I go to work both mentally and physically. I find that the more challenging the environment, the more creative and imaginative I become. After a long day of shooting in unfamiliar situations, I am often left exhausted from being in a state of high concentration for long periods of time. If I am not engaged and in my zone, I do not produce wonderful photographs… it is just that simple. Being truly engaged with the people and places you visit is a choice and the difference between creating snapshots and creating moving, interesting, and powerful travel images.

Being truly engaged with the people and places you visit is a choice.

FIELD NOTES

Connect Before You Click

When tourists enter a remote tribal village, everything changes. Welcome dances are performed and markets are erected. The youngest children are often confused by our presence and guarded from our cameras. Visitors are allowed to take as many photographs as they like, but it is often difficult to break down cultural barriers and make connections in this business-like environment. We see only what we are allowed to see and photograph only what we are allowed to photograph. We are offered a brief glimpse into another world, a snapshot of a different time and place.

On my second visit to a Samburu village in Kenya, I began working slowly and awkwardly with the market already established for my viewing. Many women remembered me from my previous visit and I was given a new name that reflected my particular aesthetic since I started shaving my head. "*Bwana Kihara*," they called me, the man with no hair or "bald guy." It was quite a joke and I began to feel more comfortable as I walked through the village. The many adults were certainly accommodating to my photographic desires, but the superficial snapshots they offered were not what I was looking for; so after shooting the market for a while, I turned my attention to the children.

I noticed a young boy playing with a home-made push toy behind a hut in the distance. As I approached with one of the village elders (his uncle), he backed away from me and had a guarded, frightened look on his face that is familiar to anyone who has seen images of poor children in Africa. The little boy I watched happily playing just moments ago was now standing perfectly still wondering who I was and what I was doing there. His uncle told me that the boy had seen very few *mzungu* (white foreigners) and had never been photographed before. His eyes were watery and red. He clearly wanted no part in my photographic cultural safari.

As I turned to photograph his uncle, I motioned for the boy to come over and look through my camera. He was reluctant and confused but found the small little window to look through while I moved the zoom in and out. He started to laugh. It was a quiet little laugh as he leaned against me and flies landed on our heads and faces. I found the shutter release with his little fingers and fired off a half dozen quick shots of his uncle. He let out a full laugh as the motor drive sounded after each shot. I had made a new friend.

While I knew that my visit and the tourist dollars we brought were helping the community, I was also challenged for the first time as a photographer by the fact that poor tribal children are not meant to be tourist attractions. I learned that to become a better photographer, I needed to make a connection before I made a photograph. Soon, several other children were asking to look through my camera and standing for portraits. Even when clearly posing for the camera, the innocent eyes of these children, uncorrupted by political indoctrination or embittered by years of hardship, drought, and hunger, expressed the spirit of a generous people.

THE RITE of PASSAGE

It was a surprisingly cool morning as we drove north out of Nairobi. I quickly began to recall the fascinating sights and smells that inspired my return to East Africa. Multitudes of people were walking and riding bicycles to and from the many markets and towns along our route. Children ran to the roadside and waved as our safari truck passed by. The profound sense of desperation I had felt the year before was considerably less intense. The long rains had finally come to most parts of Kenya after two years of drought.

The previous year I watched in shock as desperately thin cattle were dying on the roads as we casually swerved around them on our way to photograph the spectacular African wildlife. The drought, the hunger, and the sickness intensified my already unfamiliar encounters with the people and cultures of Kenya. This year I returned for a different experience. While I would certainly photograph wildlife, I came to meet and photograph two closely related nomadic tribes, the Samburu and the Maasai, who have been separated over time by hundreds of miles, yet share remarkably similar cultures and customs.

My Kikuyu guide Peter Muigai Muruthi gave our small group a quick review of current events as we continued toward our first destination, the Intrepids Lodge along the banks of the Uaso Nyiro River at the Samburu Game Reserve. We talked about our safari together last year, and we talked about the rains and the floods, the politics, and the poverty. After just a short time reminiscing with Muigai, as he prefers to be called, we turned off the main road and it was time for our journey to begin.

The Samburu are a pastoral, nomadic people. Their customs, language, and traditions are very similar to the more well-known and legendary Maasai of central and southern Kenya and northern Tanzania. There are several villages visible along the roads into the game reserve and many others just off the beaten path. Our trip was to the village of Nuguroro. The village is one of the poorest in the Samburu area. They have comparatively few real assets as measured in cattle and goats, and they see very few tourist visitors.

A typical village may have as many as twenty or thirty homes made of grasses and sticks, with thatched roofs surrounded by a thorn boma to keep out lion and hyena. The livestock is brought into the village at night after a long day grazing, which also means that there are plenty of flies around to bother tourists and photographers. Following a welcome dance, tourists are often directed to a market where bracelets, spears, gourds, blankets, carvings, and sometimes quite elaborate beadwork are available to purchase. The markets can be quite intimidating, with each individual woman vying for the opportunity to sell her personal wares.

The day we came to the village was a national holiday in Kenya. The schools were out and markets were closed, so the village was teeming with people. The pressure from women trying to sell their trinkets was intense. The children were confused by my camera and reluctant to interact, but they seemed emboldened by their sheer numbers and followed us around in large groups. It didn't take long for the excitement created by the visiting strangers to calm down. When it was clear we weren't leaving quickly, I was able to separate a few individual children from the group for portraits and grab shots around the village as they went about their business.

After a couple of hours in the village, I was now prepared to look through the makeshift tourist market. After purchasing a few items, I was

approached by a beautiful Samburu woman. She knew our visit would soon end and was aggressive to make one final sale. I was swept away and brought to the privacy of the woman's small, dark, and windowless hut to negotiate. Her baby was lying on a small piece of cowhide as she laid out several bracelets, beaded items, and little baskets for my review. After concluding my business with her, I took turns negotiating with several other women until I had spent every last shilling in my pockets.

FOLLOWING AN ENLIGHTENING AND LIVELY experience at the village, I was ready for a quick nap and an afternoon game drive. The Samburu National Park is different than the typical vision of Africa. The landscape is constantly changing, with rocky volcanic hillsides, winding rivers, large acacia trees and branched Doum palms, with endless thickets. You don't see the large herds of grazing animals in Samburu like you do at the Maasai Mara. Here everything is closer and every turn of the truck is an adventure with unexpected encounters.

At first, standing upright through the roof hatch of the Range Rover looking for animals seems strange. It is very quiet and the animals seemingly ignore our presence. Small animals like the dik dik and Thomson gazelle scurry as we approach, but the larger waterbuck, impala, gerenuk, and zebra pay no mind to the parade of tourists stopping to collect their photographs. Herds of elephants graze and the little ones play out in front of the safari trucks as if they were just another harmless African animal. You can drive for hours and very little seems to happen in Africa. Until you spot a cat. The big cats change everything.

Suddenly, a herd of grazing gerenuk or gazelle will freeze and stare off into the distance. Their heads track, slowly following some unseen danger. Somewhere out there is a hunter. Each animal knows exactly the distance required to avoid a lion attack. During the day, it is relatively easy to see and to keep this safe distance. While always alert, they are secure to graze and play while the lions sleep away the heat in some shaded, quiet spot. Since cats typically hunt at night, the best chance to spot them is in the early morning and toward dusk as they start to move to their hunting grounds.

On the morning of my second day we spotted three female lions sharing a breakfast of impala as we drove through the winding truck paths. When we arrived, the meal was almost concluded, with the

carcass consisting only of a rib cage and the head with attached spine. There was no pride anywhere to be seen, just the three hunters and their private meal. It wasn't long before the lionesses abandoned what remained of their kill and headed off, walking just feet from our truck. As they headed down the truck path, one female was calling out for the pride. We followed for over an hour as they searched for a trace. As the sun rose higher, they settled under a large acacia tree, and we moved on to photograph a family of elephants along the river before heading back to the lodge for lunch and a midday siesta.

As a tourist photographer on safari without the luxury of time, luck is always a welcomed companion. After unsuccessfully searching for the three ladies with their pride on our afternoon game drive, we spotted a leopard napping on a branch in a large tree just before sunset. We were the only truck around and had plenty of time to position for a great shot before a dozen tourist trucks crowded the scene. She moved and stretched before making a deep grunting sound that Muigai recognized as a call to a cub. Somewhere nearby was a leopard cub. We watched her for over an hour, grabbing quick shots as she turned her head into the setting sun. As we turned to leave the park for the night, we heard the cub call back from the distance.

DRIVING SOUTH THROUGH THE RIFT VALLEY from Lake Naivasha to the Maasai Mara, you begin to see the villages and cattle herds of the Maasai. The Maasai are the people of myth and legend in East Africa. They are warring pastoralists of days past who have adapted and survived in a changing environment both physically and politically. Remote villages are still very guarded and encounters can be dangerous. Photographing Maasai can be difficult.

Entering the Maasai Mara game reserve, you experience the classic vision of Africa: endless views of large herds grazing on open lands with spotty acacia trees breaking the distant horizon. The Maasai Mara National Park is a protected area just a few miles away, but with the long rains, herd animals often migrate into the reserve and graze on the short grass among the Maasai.

We arrived at the Mara near dusk with several thunderstorms visible on the horizon along the escarpment. It was truly a spectacular sight, with Maasai men driving cattle back to their villages while women repaired their rain damaged huts with fresh dung. As we approached our camp, wildebeest, zebra, and gazelle ran alongside the truck to the sound of rolling thunder. I came to visit and learn about the Maasai, but my mornings and afternoons would be spent in search of the large herds and big cats that make the Mara an important destination for the world's top wildlife photographers.

Muigai arranged our visit to a nearby Maasai village, which began with the customary welcome dance by the young men of the village. As the men performed, my attention was drawn to a group of very young boys gathered around a tree. They were mini-Maasai looking at their older brothers and fathers with a sense of awe as they performed the traditional Maasai jumping dance, called *ipid*. The little ones were stamping their feet and jumping up and down with the rhythm of the dance.

As I positioned myself to photograph the children in a genuine and spontaneous moment, they noticed me and stopped their dancing. I squatted down to photograph one of the mini-Maasai near the entry of his home when I saw through my lens a striking Maasai woman, with purpose in her stride, headed in my direction. She was graceful, confident, and very determined. I quickly refocused my camera and got off one shot before she came and gently led the small boy away from me with a quick glance of recognition that I understood to mean that the little ones were off limits.

My experience with the Maasai was much different than those I had with the more remote Samburu. The confused children at Samburu, however guarded, allowed me to capture a glimpse of their life and a sense of their struggle. The uncomfortable and intense situations in the towns and the forced portraits I negotiated earlier in my trip seemed so much more real to me now. The Maasai were prepared for my visit and were not going to open their world to me at this time or in this place. Instead, they gave me their show.

That afternoon, a little disappointed in myself for not getting classic images that would reveal the essence of being Maasai, we set out on our last game drive following two male lions, thinking we had been very lucky in all that we had seen. Countless times in the Mara, I have watched as various herds of game seemingly spring to attention whenever an animal is spooked by something unseen in the high grass. When lions are spotted or are seen walking in the distance, the wildebeest, gazelle, topi, zebra, and even the giraffe remain very still, constantly monitoring the position of the deadly predator until they are a safe distance away.

There is very little on the plains of Africa that will intimidate a healthy lion, but remarkably, the lions we had been following sharply reversed direction and slowly headed for the cover of a thicket. Surprised by this, we went with them. A short time later, two small red dots appeared on the horizon. It was the *shuka* (cloth wrap worn by the Maasai) of two Maasai men walking across the open plains of the Mara on their way to market. The top predator on the plains of East Africa is not the lion, it is the Maasai. Or more accurately, was the Maasai.

For hundreds of years, the Maasai hunted lions as the rite of passage to manhood and to protect their herds of cattle. It has been decades since they stopped routinely killing lions, but generations of lions are still conditioned to avoid them. The lions we followed knew well before us that Maasai were nearby and quietly moved away until they were at a safe distance under cover. In an area where most humans would certainly be a quick and easy meal for a lion, the Maasai walk without fear or hesitation. Muigai said the lion somehow know the Maasai, probably by smell, and can identify them at long distances. After dark the tables are turned and the Maasai surrender the African night and retreat to the safety of their village and their impenetrable thorn boma.

OPPOSITE PAGE: Birethanti, Nepal

Chapter 2
Local Lifestyles

"Photography is the only 'language' understood in all parts of the world, and bridging all nations and cultures."

—Helmut Gernsheim

As a traveler, it is inevitable that you will encounter customs and cultures that are different from your own, and sometimes even inconsistent with your values. For some, exploring our cultural differences is a big part of why they travel. But for most tourists, being far from home is a state of being that challenges them both physically and emotionally. Different foods, languages, traditions, and unrecognizable surroundings can be an intimidating part of the travel experience. The more exotic or different the local lifestyle than your own, the more likely you are to be captivated or repulsed by unusual or unfamiliar traditions.

Learning about and photographing how others live also involves carefully navigating a myriad of cultural mores. What is considered normal back home can be quite inappropriate abroad. Some cultures might forgive, or even laugh at, our silly tourist *faux pas*, but others might take offense and find our behavior terribly insulting. In a broader sense, we truly are guests in another person's home. Being a responsible tourist means making ourselves aware of the consequences of our actions and traveling with empathy and respect for all that makes us different and unique.

Angle of View

Novice photographers tend to photograph the world from eye-level, creating predictable images. Sometimes, squatting down will help you avoid a distraction in the background or getting up higher will let you crop out unwanted elements. Those are practical reasons to find a different camera angle, but finding a unique way to photograph a scene can dramatically affect a viewer's emotional reaction to an image.

An unfamiliar or unexpected way of looking at something confuses our visual cues and can create surprise, interest, and curiosity in your photographs. Low angles exaggerate height and perspective, while looking down on a subject can provide context to complicated scenes. This may require you to lie on the ground, crawl, or climb to find a different angle of view, but the effort will result in a new look at a familiar scene. When you are stuck for an idea, squat down and look again.

People to People

One of the challenges when traveling with a large tour group is the resulting fishbowl effect. Tour groups often parade around as a pack or witness local life from the window of a bus or van on their way to the next attraction. The fishbowl effect perpetuates the "us and them" of tourism by inhibiting people-to-people interactions. From a distance it is very hard to capture images of the local lifestyle or have meaningful interactions, especially in poor or developing countries. Unfortunately, tourists are also often viewed from a distance as a necessary evil that creates jobs or generates local revenue.

Often smaller, more intimate tours will provide opportunities for locals and foreigners to interact in ways that are authentic, honorable, relevant, and contemporary. If yours does not, you can plan your trip around a local festival or cultural event or make the most of your few precious moments of alone time to wander to the edge of town, photograph a local sporting event, street market, or people at work.

Of course the main tourist attractions of your chosen destination will be the highlights of your tour, but equally enjoyable moments, and wonderful photographs, can come from meet-

OPPOSITE PAGE LEFT TO RIGHT: Beijing, China; Chichicastenango, Guatemala

ing people at a small café while sampling the local coffees or trying a new beer at a local pub. Following a long day of sightseeing, it is tempting to go directly from the bus to the bed, but there is often a doorway to a special memory open just a few minutes away from your hotel.

The adorable little girl dressed in traditional clothing wandering the streets of Cuzco in Peru carrying a baby lamb is working!

Beware of the Cute Kid with a Baby Lamb

The natural curiosity of children makes them a great way to start shooting and find your comfort zone in an unfamiliar place. Groups of children at play in a safe environment surrounded by family in a town or village will not be afraid to approach a curious stranger. If there are adults nearby, acknowledge them as you take your first shots of the kids. When they see that you are playful and not a threat, you will have more freedom to explore. Once you start showing the kids their images in the back of the camera, you will have new friends.

Children are often a wonderful bridge across a cultural divide, but one reality that travelers must always be aware of is that in many places around the world, tourists are their targets. Not targets of violence, but targets for your money.

When tourists are spotted, beggars, hawkers, and scammers seem to show up quickly and in many forms. The adorable little girl dressed in traditional clothing wandering the streets of Cuzco in Peru carrying a baby lamb is working! She is so cute it is hard not to take her picture, but she will expect to be paid, often aggressively, and her mother is most certainly watching nearby.

Paying for portraits is a difficult topic for both professional and tourist photographers alike. I do on occasion discreetly offer a token of thanks to someone for letting me take his or her picture, but I never pay the cute kid with a lamb or her equivalent in different parts of the world. The shots are rarely cute and authenticity is virtually impossible to achieve. No doubt her family could use the money, but in this instance both the tourist and the local community are being exploited.

Don't be fooled by this Hmong tribal cutie I encountered at Wat Prathat Doi Suthep in Chiang Mai, Thailand…she was working. A moment after snapping this shot, her hand went out. I said, "No money." She said, in her practiced English and with a scowl now on her adorable face, "No money… no picture."

BELOW: Namibia
OPPOSITE PAGE: Tangulbei, Kenya

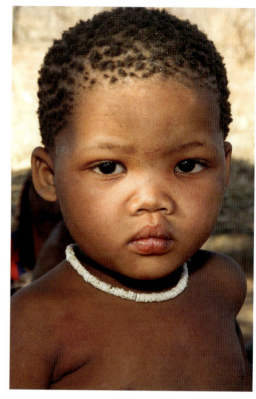

Most importantly, if young children become an important source of income for the family through begging from tourists or being paid for pictures, it is unlikely that they will ever attend school, condemning them to a life of poverty.

If you do choose to offer a thank you token to an adult, discretion is the key word. Never pull out your wallet and openly hand over cash before or after a portrait, unless taking the picture was part of a negotiated event. If I really want to photograph someone who clearly wants to be paid, I will often nod my head up and down (a universal form of agreement), take my pictures, then approach my subject to show them an image. After showing them their portrait, I take or shake their hand, saying "thank you" with a small token of appreciation tucked in my palm. Understand that overtly paying for portraits contributes to a culture that will create an expectation for the next group of tourists that comes along.

Indigenous Tourism

"Do you still throw spears at each other?" was the unfortunate question posed by a high-profile figure not so many years ago. "No, we don't do that any more" was the beautifully spontaneous reply of William Brim, the founder of Tjapukai, an aboriginal culture park in Queensland, Australia. The question may have been intended as humor or as a light-hearted comment, but it does illustrate an all-too-often expressed value

Pokot Encounter

On the way west across the Rift Valley in Kenya, our guide pulled off the road in an area called Tangulbei—Pokot country. Within a minute or two we could hear the beating of drums in the distance. The Pokot knew we had stopped. Our guide found a young boy who spoke Swahili and told him that we wished to photograph some of the women who had come to meet us. After our models were selected and fees negotiated, the women just stood perfectly still and expressionless posing for snapshots and anxious to get back to what they were doing before we entered their world. It was a strange and uncomfortable encounter for all of us.

I found an older woman with a time-weathered face and a sizable dent in her forehead. Her beaded jewelry was faded and her tribal clothing tattered and worn. She had clearly lived a long, hard life in the African bush. Children were playfully gathering as I worked with my confused and hesitant model. I inquired about her name and had our guide ask our translator to ask my model to smile for me. As the language was changed and my message delivered, the crowd of Pokot around us broke out in laughter, and I had my shot of the beautiful woman with a full and toothless smile.

Point of View

Don't mistake the "angle of view" with "point of view." Point of view is an attitude or opinion. In photography it is the position of the photographer in relation to the scene and a particular way of seeing or considering the events depicted.

Voyeur – implies that the participants don't know that we are watching. There is tension created by the sense that we are sneaking a peak at an event we were not invited to witness.

Spectator – the participants know they are being watched and photographed. The viewer has a sense that they are a part of the crowd witnessing an event as it unfolds.

Objective Observer – a recording of a scene as a detached witness. The photographer avoids a point of view that implies they are actively participating in the event depicted. No eye contact, no strong perspective, typically shot from eye level, with a normal focal-length lens.

Likewise, as a viewer of a photograph we assume the point of view of the photographer. Are we a spectator, voyeur, objective observer, or participant? Each point of view has clues that communicate how the viewer is intended to interpret the image. Successful photographs are experienced on several levels, and successful photographers consciously choose a point of view to elicit a response. Altering your point of view is a great way to change the narrative of your pictures.

Participant – places the viewer into the action of the scene. Great for crowded or tight places where the viewer has a sense that they are there.

OPPOSITE PAGE CLOCKWISE: Tibet; Thailand; Tokyo, Japan; Paris, France
LEFT: Negev Desert, Israel

judgment of so-called primitive cultures by travelers from so-called civilized nations.

When we travel we also bring with us our view of the world as understood through our own particular cultural lens. Nowhere is the tourist fishbowl effect of "us" and "them" so clearly evident as in cultural and indigenous tourism. Today, the tribal myth, or the vision of primitive cultures living in harmony with nature, maintains and drives the ethno-tourism product for many countries. The tribal experience is often incorporated into their national destination branding. For indigenous tourists, the tribal experience also seems to satisfy our romantic desire to search for unadulterated peoples threatened by the evil advance of modernity.

Indigenous tourism, including visits to remote tribes, schools, and orphanages, can be some of our most rewarding and lasting tourist memories. But a tourist experience at the expense of others in my opinion is irresponsible. We often leave with a warm and fuzzy feeling after an experience playing with the world's "cute" tribal children, but for many of these kids, there is nothing cute about their lives. All over the world poor tribal children are destined to live a life of poverty with the occasional visit from a rich foreigner. By their teenage years, the cute kids have often become resentful and distrusting of tourists.

The tribal communities tourists visit today have chosen to enter the tourism industry. They have chosen to allow us to enter their homes and villages, in exchange for our money. It is important, however, to enable true connections that are not simply financial transactions for us to witness their culture from afar, but that are culturally sensitive and benefit the host communities in multiple ways.

When done right, indigenous tourism is much more than marketing buzzwords or product offerings. It is about sharing an intimate knowledge of a culture and unique way of life through song, dance, and story. It is about a genuine interaction between different worldviews, bridging the gap between cultures and generations, and it is about developing a mutual respect for our common humanity. Mutually beneficial relationships are essential for the sustainability of indigenous tourism. Travelers who can genuinely connect with the people and places they visit will be transformed through cultural experiences.

A Wild Ride

Local communities have domesticated and tamed animals for centuries as a source of food, hunting partner, companion, and beast of burden. Of all the animals we have lived and worked with, only a few have been used as transportation. Camels, horses, elephants, even yaks and llamas, have been incorporated into tourist

adventures all over the world. Many destinations offer riding tours specific to their particular location. Each provides its own thrill and inherent discomfort, while offering a different perspective of the local culture.

For desert people in areas of India, the Middle East, North Africa, and the caravan routes of the ancient Silk Road, the camel has historically been vital to their very survival. The camel was, and for many still is, a lifeline of the people, not only providing a ride, but also milk, meat, leather, and wool. Nomadic desert tribes have forged a special bond with the camel, and their traditional economy depends on the produce of the faithful mount. For a tourist, even a brief camel ride can expose a unique way of life and the important relationship between an animal and a desert culture. It can also be the only way to see and photograph some of the most starkly beautiful landscapes on earth.

Likewise, the Asian elephant has played an important role in the creation of the modern Thai nation. Historically, the elephant transported goods and people and worked in the forestry and agriculture industries that fueled Thailand's industrialization and modernization. In 1989 the Thai government banned all logging in protected areas. The collapse of the logging industry left a large number of *mahouts* (the keeper or driver of an elephant) with no way to pay for the expensive care and support of their elephants. They turned to tourism.

Today, more than half of Thailand's elephants work in the tourism industry. Without the tourist camps, many of these beautiful giants would not survive. But do your homework. Elephant riding is popular in other countries in Southeast Asia, Nepal, and many areas of India. It is also very controversial and protested by animal rights organizations because of the illegal trade of young elephants, who are sometimes mistreated with bullhooks and electric prods during their training. There are certainly many well-run, responsible elephant camps and riding tours, so be an educated tourist if you choose to mount one of these amazing creatures.

OPPOSITE PAGE: Kalaw, Myanmar
BELOW LEFT TO RIGHT: Chiang Rai, Thailand; Phuket, Thailand; Rajasthan, India

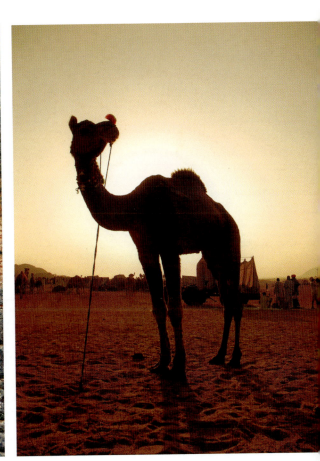

Local Lifestyles

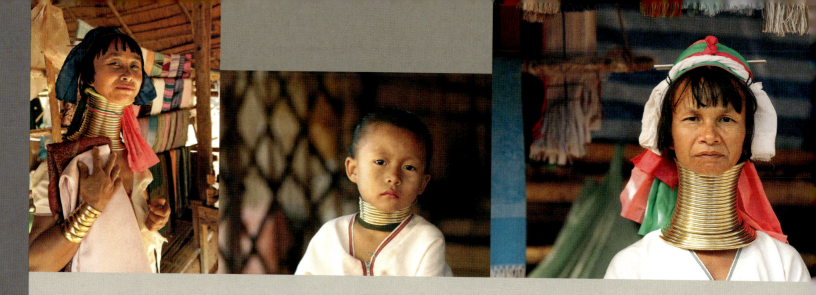

FIELD NOTES

A Hill Tribe Spectacle

As human beings, we are both repelled and inextricably attracted to the unfamiliar, the strange, and the seemingly incomprehensible. Like so many visitors to Thailand, I, too, felt drawn to visit the long-necked women of the northern hill tribes, knowing full well that the images I captured might perpetuate the stereotypes and devalue the very culture that fascinated me.

I have been struggling to comprehend the vagaries and challenges of cultural tourism and the commodification of the tribal experience for over a decade. This struggle achieved a new level of complexity for me when I was introduced to a young girl who faces a potential life of humiliation and deformity because her family was lucky enough to escape starvation, war, and genocide. Her name is Mookbai and she is six years old. She is part of a community commonly referred to as "long-neck Karen."

The Karen is one of the largest hill tribes in Southeast Asia with many subgroups and cultural variations. One subgroup of the Karen, the

Kayan tribe from the border region of Myanmar (Burma) and Thailand, is believed to have migrated from Mongolia during the Bronze Age and is best known for the brass neck rings worn by their women. Mookbai was the first villager I encountered as I approached their collection of huts, set among trees and separated by a dusty path. Upon seeing me, she quickly turned and disappeared into the village maze.

There is no exact time, no predetermined waiting period before the tribal women who work the tourist markets around the world let down their guard, but it always happens. After hours in the village, it was clear that I was not a typical tourist. I played with the kids and hung out with the women between visits by tour groups. The young girls gathered and giggled. Groups of women sang traditional songs accompanied by an old guitar, and many simply sat quietly at their handlooms making the beautiful scarves that are their primary source of income. It was a happy village, and I felt free to explore.

As one tour group approached, the women and children once again returned to their respective huts and to their assorted products for sale. They smiled their dutiful smiles as cameras and smartphones violated

FIELD NOTES

their personal space. The groups, led by a tour guide, crowded the women, gawking and laughing. The guides often touched the women as they explained the curiosities on display. Several times Kayan women glanced over at me. I could sense their humiliation but had nothing more to offer than an empathetic smile. No doubt they experience this humiliation every day, but it was clearly different with me as a witness.

It would be easy to decry the people and circumstances that created this situation, but their story is more complicated than that. In the late 1980s and early 1990s many Karen tribes fled to the Thailand border to escape war and genocide in Myanmar. They came as refugees and live with an uncertain legal status. The lucky ones, they say, have relocated to simulated villages where scores of curious tourists, both foreign and domestic, gawk at and photograph the unfamiliar. The Thai authorities consider these tourist villages self-sustaining refugee camps. They have some land for farming, earn money by selling their handicrafts, and their children are educated in local schools.

After a while, Mookbai was following me around, fascinated by her image in the back of my digital camera. I had made a new friend and was touched by the gentleness of this beautiful little girl. Traditionally, Kayan girls are fitted with rings at the age of five or six. The process continues with successive rings being added every couple years. Over time the weight of these rings crushes their collarbones and deforms their clavicle giving the appearance of a grotesquely stretched neck. The women of the village clearly understand that it is this unusual practice that is attracting tourists and the tourist dollars now necessary to sustain their village.

It is a tradition, however, that younger generations of women who live in Myanmar and the refugee camps of Thailand have increasingly rejected. I couldn't help but wonder if my visit and my tourist dollars, while providing some short-term good, might also condemn Mookbai to a life as a tourist spectacle. I am told that at seven years of age, the Kayan kids enter government schools and mainstream with other Thai children. Many girls do choose to take off the rings before the deformity is irreversible. Will Mookbai have that option?

There are no easy answers when dealing with people struggling to meet the needs of their families—only more difficult questions to propose. It is hard to suspend judgment when confronted with ancient traditions that don't seem to have a place in our modern world. What we can do, I believe, is travel with empathy, understanding, and kindness. We can be drawn to the unfamiliar, patronize their tourist villages, and hopefully leave with a genuine appreciation for a different culture where the people we meet can retain their dignity.

CHINA'S NEW SILK ROAD

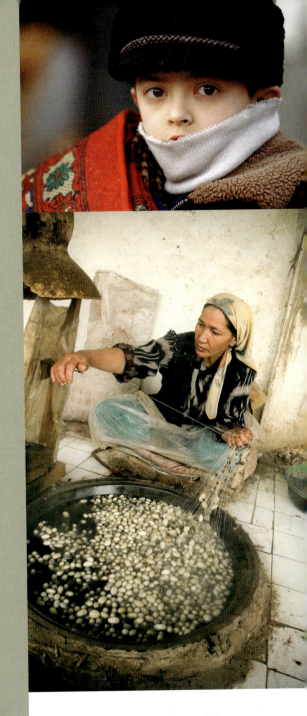

Just hours after arriving in the ancient city of Kashgar, via a late-night plane out of Urumqi, I was amidst throngs of worshipers outside Id Kah Mosque in the predawn darkness.

Romantic images of remote oases, exotic bazaars, and camel caravans laden with precious stones, spices, and shimmering silks crossing the vast unforgiving desert flickered in and out of my consciousness as I wandered alone in front of the historic yellow-tiled mosque. I was a bit dazed and confused after traveling continuously for three days, journeying halfway around the world to be transported to what seemed several centuries back in time.

As I waited for morning prayers to begin, I was quickly engulfed in an eerily quiet sea of black overcoats and fur hats as thousands of men gathered slowly and deliberately in front of the mosque. My long journey to Kashgar was intended to coincide with the Muslim Festival of Sacrifice, Eid al-Adha, which marks the end of the annual Muslim pilgrimage (Hajj). As a westerner and non-Muslim, I was thrilled and humbled to witness this ancient tradition,

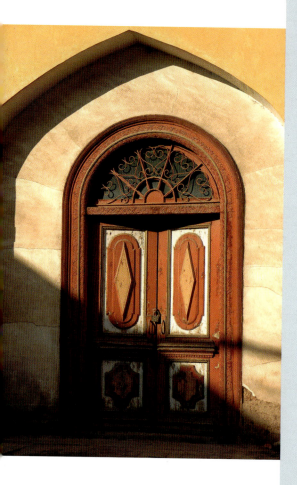

which symbolizes a willingness to make sacrifices in order to stay on the Straight Path.

My group was invited to join a large extended Uyghur (pronounced Wee-gurr) family for their annual feast in an ancient section of this increasingly modern city. I watched as a young lamb was presented in the trellised courtyard of their mud-brick home and slaughtered in a solemn ritual that dated back centuries; its body twitching as the sharp blade opened its throat, creating a flow of blood that quickly filled a large ceramic bowl as its executioner whispered a prayer and caressed its dying body.

The children ran and played joyfully as the men attended to the slaughter and the women went about making preparations for the holiday meal. The strange mix of faces and the unfamiliar sights, sounds, and smells all conspired to transform a place of antiquity into a complex living history that left me emotionally exhausted and overwhelmed. I had never before felt so completely foreign or so far from home.

IN THE TWO DAYS THAT FOLLOWED the festival, thousands of sheep, goat, and lamb skins were piled high in the streets. The sweet smoky odor of grilled mutton and cumin saturated the cool breeze as I walked along Aizirete Lu near the famous Yengi Bazaar. Bicycles, motorcycles, taxis, buses, and donkey carts weaved through the mass of pedestrians. Veiled women mingled among scores of men adorned with intricately embroidered skullcaps, traditional to the Uyghur of Chinese Turkistan.

Every Sunday, the streets of Kashgar swell by fifty thousand people as the entire community gathers at one of Asia's liveliest markets. Tribes of Tajiks, Kazakhs, and Uzbeks from nearby mountain villages blend into the human mosaic with Pakistani traders and tourists from around the world. The wide boulevards are lined with vendors selling kabobs, dumplings, and *nang* bread baked in earthen ovens. Nearby, the famous Sunday market goes under cover as endless fluorescent-lit stalls bulge with clothing, hats, footwear, electronics, knives, silks, pashmina, and assorted tourist trinkets.

The products have changed over time, but the scene is not new to this fabled city. Two thousand years ago, the three ancient caravan routes of the Silk Road converged at Kashgar. Multiethnic traders and herdsmen dressed in the unique costumes of their homelands bartered over the vendibles of antiquity. Travelers to the region told stories of remote oases, exotic bazaars, and camel caravans crossing the

Taklamakan Desert. But what stirs the imagination and ignites romantic interest in the Silk Road are not the historic accounts of trade and commerce along its great length, but the symbolic and metaphorical impact of centuries of cultural exchange.

Near the borders with Kyrgyzstan, Afghanistan, Tajikistan, and Pakistan, Kashgar holds a strategic position between the Pamir Mountains to the west and Taklamakan Desert to the east. During its two millennia of existence, this oasis town on the edge of modern China has been ruled by countless tribes and influenced by European, Islamic, Persian, Mongolian, and Chinese cultures. Kashgar was at the crossroads of the world's great religions, foods, music and dance, and each left something of itself behind.

By the fifteenth century, Islam had become the dominant religion throughout the entire Taklamakan region. As the overland trade routes of the past gave way to the sea, desert towns and villages became increasingly shut off from the outside world. Under the Ming Dynasty (1368–1644), the Silk Road was abandoned by China, further isolating the once-flourishing communities. Only the largest and best-watered oases survived the advance of invading sands. Today, the Turkic-speaking Central Asian people known as Uyghur claim this desolate land as their ancestral home.

Both Kashgar and the regional capital of Urumqi have profited greatly from the New Silk Road and the "Develop the West" initiative launched out of Beijing. In recent years, improved infrastructure and accommodations, as well as the potential for great profit, have attracted a virtual flood of traders, investors, and tourists from around the world to the westernmost city in China and the major oasis towns of the Xinjiang Uyghur Autonomous Region as a new form of globalization sweeps across the region.

In the larger cities of Xinjiang, the dusty streets of mud-brick houses, once overflowing with donkey carts, are being replaced by the sprawl of globalism in the form of concrete, glass, and steel. The old neighborhoods of Kashgar are slowly being squeezed, while the towering 79-foot (24-m) statue of Chairman Mao is a constant reminder of the enduring complexity of this ancient crossroad between China and Central Asia.

WHILE KASHGAR HAS BEEN WELCOMING foreigners for thousands of years, it is no longer a remote outpost of civilization in one of the harshest landscapes on earth. Located at a natural intersection connecting overland pathways from China and Mongolia in the east to the ancient capitals of Rome, Persia, and Babylon in the west, Kashgar has been a historic meeting place of cultures and ideas for millennia. On multiple trips, I used the increasingly accessible city as a point of entry to explore the Karakoram Highway to Taxkorgan (Tashkorgan) and the two routes of the ancient Silk Road that skirt the edges of the Tarim Basin to the north and south of the Taklamakan Desert.

For centuries, the caravan path that is now the newly paved 250-mile (400-km) Karakoram Highway was used by travelers of the Silk Road between Islamabad and Kashgar through the Khunjerab Pass. It is here that four of the world's great mountain ranges converge on China's western border to form the Pamir Highland, and it was through this gateway that a young Marco Polo entered China in the late thirteenth century on his way east along the Silk Road to visit the Mongol Emperor Kublai Khan in what is now Beijing.

During the time of Polo, the area was inhabited by hordes of bandits who took advantage of the terrain to plunder caravans traveling through the valley. He described them as "idolaters and utter savages, living entirely by the chase and dressed in the skins of beast." The barbarous tribes no longer exist, but the Pamir Highland remains a sparsely populated and barren land. The nearly thirty thousand seminomadic Muslim Tajiks who now occupy the 13,123-foot-high (4,000-m) valley live in low mud-brick houses that blend seamlessly into the landscape and provide an effective shelter against the bitter cold. They herd their livestock and subsistence-farm in a beautiful but unforgiving place.

While there is still some debate about whether or not Marco Polo actually made the journey or visited all the places he chronicles in his circa-1298 book *Description of the World*, he does describe many lakes, rivers, and mountains familiar to modern travelers on the Karakoram Highway. He writes of an arduous twelve-day odyssey before resting briefly in Kashgar, and heading south on an eight-day journey along the southern route of the Silk Road to Hotan.

When I finally reached Hotan on my summer tour of the southern route, I was desperately ill. Something I had eaten didn't agree with me. Regardless of the source, I felt truly awful as we visited one of the most legendary cities of the ancient Silk Road. Following a long and particularly forgettable night, I slept all morning on our minibus as the rest of my group toured a modern silk factory on the outskirts of town. By mid-afternoon I was feeling much better and thoroughly enjoyed our visit to a traditional center of Aidelis silk production and the large bazaar at the heart of the city.

After shopping the bazaar and shooting some of the local landmarks, I left Hotan on the final stage of my journey across the Taklamakan Desert on the newly completed Cross-Desert Highway. I found that historic places with romantic names such as Yengisar, Yarkand, Hotan, and Niya (Minfeng) that were once important centers of international trade have been nearly forgotten by the wave of globalism that is poised to bring great prosperity to the New Silk Road.

Outside of the major cities of Xinjiang, the promised prosperity is much harder to see. The bazaars and livestock markets look much like they must have centuries ago, while jade is still harvested and sold along with traditional handmade silk in isolated villages alive with authenticity and simplicity. Donkey carts loaded with produce line the highways en route to the Sunday market as trucks and buses sound their presence with the blare of deafening horns.

Many of the communities confined to the small patches of green, precariously situated between the world's second largest desert and the Kulun Mountains of the Tibetan plateau, predate marauding armies, feuding tribes, and Venetian travel writers. For centuries, the east-west flow of goods along the great trans-Asian highway was entirely dependent upon the fragile line of isolated oases conveniently located no more than a couple days' travel across the shifting sands of the suffocating desert. Without these life-giving islands to sustain the traders, merchants, and herdsmen of the commercial caravans, the ancient Silk Road would not have flourished or even existed.

Ironically, the New Silk Road offers modern businessmen great opportunities to exploit the vast natural and human resources of western China; yet these twenty-first century industrialists no longer need to rest and water their beasts at the tiny oasis towns that cling to the edge of relevance. No longer do individuals from different tribes, countries, or cultures need to barter and negotiate face-to-face in crowded bazaars. High-tech products and today's essential commodities of oil and steel drive, fly, or flow right by, due to the massive investment in infrastructure and pipelines that define a new era.

While the Silk Road remains a symbolic representation of the interconnectedness of multiethnic and multinational cultures, it is easy to forget that China's legendary oases are still home to a vibrant community of people caught between their ancient traditions and their modern aspirations. Their culture, exhibited through song and dance, still entertains weary travelers, and their exotic spices, precious stones, and silks continue to attract buyers from distant lands. But today, their bazaars are surveyed by tourists searching for a simple souvenir in this new form of cultural exchange.

nepal
THROUGH INNOCENT EYES

I could hear him coming as I glanced across the room of my trekkers lodge. The pale green numbers of my alarm clock were glowing 5:37 in the darkness. "The mountain is clear, the mountain is clear," whispered our guide Raju in a voice so soft it seemed intended to awaken us without actually disturbing our sleep.

After a few more stolen moments of rest, I dragged myself out of bed to find five peaks of the Annapurna range visible as shadows against the soft blue, predawn sky. I walked down a small hill toward a clearing where a group of campers were breaking down their tents as the sun slowly topped the jagged horizon and the summit of Annapurna South began to glow a pale yellow. The first light of day danced across the peaks, separating the mountains from the sky. The foothills in the foreground distinguished themselves in different shades of blue and black. It was as if I could just reach across the Modi valley and touch the snow-capped mountains.

I had been on the trail for several days with a small group of fellow Americans. The rugged terrain and hours of navigating steep stone steps had become a familiar part of our daily routine. After packing our gear and eating breakfast, we set off on a path through the village of Ghandruk following Raju and the young porters who carried our heavy loads through the mountains in baskets (*doko*) on their backs, anchored to their foreheads by a simple strap.

As we began our trek, the village of mud and stone came alive with activity. Women were starting their day with routine chores, while dogs

and chickens cleared the stone walkway in advance of the passing parade of tourist trekkers. Children played in the cobblestone streets as mule trains hauling propane and rice navigated the narrow alleyways. Around every corner we experienced another breathtaking view of village life set against the spectacular mountain backdrop.

Whenever we neared a village, children came out to greet us, nearly as excited as we were, shouting "Namaste… Namaste," the traditional Hindu greeting. Namaste was quickly followed by "hello" and "school pen," a small bit of English that has spread throughout the Nepali mountain network like a viral video on YouTube. Raju grew up in this area and knew many people along the trail. It was fun to watch him interact with the small boys who looked up to him as a hero who can speak the language of the wealthy.

The stone paths we were walking are the highways of the Middle Hills, connecting generations of mountain people to an ever-increasing number of foreigners. Through these trails a new generation of Nepali children are being introduced to a new form of cultural exchange with strangers from around the world, dressed in hi-tech fabrics and armed with trekking poles and digital cameras. For some it is clearly overwhelming, but for many children these newcomers to their mountain villages are an irresistible curiosity.

IN THIS SEEMINGLY IDYLLIC RURAL LANDSCAPE where terraced slopes and primitive farming methods provide stunning photo opportunities, it is easy to believe that the communities that live in these verdant hills are prosperous. But the farmers who work the tiny terraced farm plots of the Middle Hills barely raise enough food to support their own families. Much of the arable land has been cropped continuously since the twelfth century, forcing farmers to cut a living from steeper

and more fragile slopes. Throughout the hills there are abandoned terraces exhausted of the mineral nutrients necessary for continued farming.

Nearly 80 percent of Nepal's people live in rural areas where the economy is dominated by subsistence agriculture. Increasingly, families own a small piece of land where they attempt to earn a living and enough extra food to sell at the nearest market in exchange for household necessities like sugar, salt, soap, and cloth to make clothing. But there remain remnants of a feudal system, where tenant farmers share their small harvest with landowners of higher castes. Population growth has also put pressure on limited resources and forced many men to leave their farms for Nepal's major cities or cross the border into India in search of work.

Further complicating Nepal's social fabric is a population of nearly thirty million, made up of hundreds of distinct ethnic communities, races, tribes, castes, and subcastes, speaking dozens of different languages and dialects. The many customs and traditions of the three major migrations from Tibet, India, and Central Asia that populated Nepal have been intermingled, but the wealth and spoils of political power have largely been restricted to the rulers of the Kathmandu Valley while the high mountain passes are a crossroad for pilgrims and traders between China and India.

In early 1951, Nepal's King Tribhuvan ousted the hereditary family of prime ministers known as the Ranas, who were the de facto rulers of the country for centuries, and Nepal cautiously began to welcome outsiders. After centuries as a cloistered Hindu kingdom, shrouded in mystery on the roof of the world, the first westerners in over a hundred years began arriving in Kathmandu to establish political relationships and climb her lofty peaks.

As Nepal gradually welcomed outsiders, remote mountain villages were connected with larger market economies, but Nepal entered the modern world with a twelfth-century infrastructure. Following decades of failed governments and unsuccessful attempts at democratic reform, frustration and hopelessness spread from the cities to the countryside. The poverty of peasant farmers, high unemployment in cities, often oppressive treatment of women and ethnic minorities, combined with the lack of opportunity, gave rise to the Maoist movement in 1996 known as "The People's War."

DESPITE BILLIONS OF DOLLARS IN MILITARY AID to the Royal Nepal Army from the British and United States governments, the Maoist insurgency continued to grow in the early years of the new millennium. Their ranks swelled with poor villagers from the mountains and hills who believed they were fighting for a cause. The insurrection targeted so-called "enemies of the people" and forcibly shut down many government services, effectively closing rural schools and leaving an entire generation without an education. With nearly half of Nepal's population under the age of sixteen, it was just a matter of time before children were recruited from the caste of "untouchables" as spies, laborers, and killers.

The tipping point of the insurgency came in February 2005 when King Gyanendra declared a state of emergency and seized absolute power. In opposition, the seven major political parties of Nepal united with the insurgent Maoists in an alliance against the monarchy. In April 2006, they organized massive countrywide demonstrations, forcing the king to reinstate parliament. Within days, the Maoists declared a unilateral ceasefire and began peace talks with the new government. The triumphant movement resulted in the reported deaths of nearly thirteen thousand police, military, insurgents, and civilians between 1996 and 2006.

Following a comprehensive peace agreement and the constituent assembly elections in 2008, which saw the Maoists emerge as the leading party, congress abolished the monarchy, ending two hundred forty years of royal rule. The portrait of dethroned King Gyanendra was replaced on bank notes with an image of Mount Everest, and the Royal Palace in Kathmandu became a public museum.

The year after the ceasefire witnessed a new wave of tourism to the beleaguered country. Despite a worldwide economic slowdown, tourism has continued to grow, rivaling Nepal's peak years before the war. Guides and outfitters who left the country have returned, and new lodging is being created along the major trekking circuits, but the transition is not complete. The People's War has ended, but the fight to become a unified nation will continue for years to come.

THE SOUNDS OF DISTANT DOGS BARKING and roosters crowing broke the chatter of countless birds. Hearing "the mountain is clear, the mountain is clear" brought a smile to my face as I prepared for my last day of trekking in Nepal. Our group set out early for the small village of Tanchok before trekking out to Lumle to begin our journey home. Raju told us that the village was once home to a large group of Gurkha soldiers, the legendary fighters that continue to serve in the British and Indian armies.

As we neared the village, we were once again met by a small group of kids and a chorus of "Namaste." But something was different. The houses were lifeless and apparently abandoned. The village looked run-down, gritty, and old. Many of the buildings were in need of repair, and fewer people were around, compared to the many villages we had trekked through in recent days.

We encountered two older women sitting on the ground weaving fabric into a quilt. They smiled at our arrival. One woman immediately asked Raju for some ointment for her sore back, which he didn't hesitate to provide. We learned that there are fifty-five families living in the village, but many had migrated to the cities. Most of the soldiers who once lived here have moved to the UK with a good army pension. The women seemed happy to share their stories and have a bit of unexpected company. They said that very few visitors came by there anymore.

Before leaving the village, I noticed an old woman who wore the years of hard labor and struggle on her face. She was carrying a young girl in her arms. It had been a long and rewarding trip, but I knew this would be my last chance to capture one more memory of Nepal and maybe end the day with a happy story to share. I walked toward them and pointed to my camera. Once again I was greeted with two more smiles and another "Namaste" from a beautiful child.

Since the ceasefire of 2006, Nepal has given birth to a new generation facing new challenges, but now with open doors inviting people from around the world to walk the stone steps of their mountain villages. Nepal is a country that can only truly be appreciated on foot. Distances are not measured in miles or kilometers, but in how many hours or days it will take to walk to your destination. There is no easy way to experience the magic of these mountains. For that, travelers need to follow in the footsteps of Nepal's people, taking one step at a time on a path with no end.

While the scars of a bloody conflict remain, the young boys and girls of Nepal's Middle Hills are being introduced to a world without guns, bombs, and killing. It is a world where polyester and pashmina coexist with Gore-Tex and yak wool. Fear and violence are being replaced with a new language of friendship, and tourist trekkers from around the world are learning about the hopes and dreams of a nation, through the innocent eyes of her children.

OPPOSITE PAGE: Negev Desert, Israel

Chapter 3
Where People Gather

"Your eye must see a composition or an expression that life itself offers you, and you must know with intuition when to click the camera."

—Henri Cartier-Bresson

Just about everyone has tried to take pictures of people they meet on their journeys. Often they are shot quickly, candidly, and from a distance to avoid the uncomfortable feelings we get when approaching someone we don't know. It is natural to be uncomfortable photographing strangers in a strange land, but shooting portraits can be the most fulfilling and rewarding part of the tourist experience.

There is nothing more difficult for a tourist than capturing an authentic human connection in a photograph. It takes courage to raise your camera in a crowded street market or approach a stranger in an unfamiliar country to ask for a picture. If you do, for one brief moment in time you are connected with another human being and sharing an experience that transcends cultural differences. To make great photographs of people, you need to go where people gather.

A Gift from Innocent Eyes

In the late 1990s, while working as an advertising photographer, I was offered a special assignment to photograph several cigar manufacturing facilities in Bahia, Brazil. It was my first trip outside of the United States and Canada, and it revealed a different, grittier reality than I had ever experienced. The abundance of new sights and smells was overwhelming.

As we traveled between locations, I had the opportunity to wander through some small towns and photograph scenes of daily life. A young girl crossing a narrow cobblestone street noticed me at the same moment she caught my eye. She stopped a short distance away, her faint smile hidden behind two bags she held near her face. I pointed to the camera in my hand and she offered permission with a slight nod of her head. I fired off a couple shots and we went our separate ways.

This was long before digital photography, so I left Brazil with a couple hundred rolls of unprocessed transparency film. I spent days going through slide after slide looking for those images of my chance encounter. I still remember the rush of adrenaline when I set my magnifying lupe on the image of that little girl. Her eyes were captivating. Her gentle gaze exposed a graceful innocence.

As photographers, we talk a lot about shots that we have "taken" or a shot that I "took," but this image wasn't anything I took from that little girl…it was a gift that she gave to me. Each person grants permission in their own way and sometimes no matter how politely you ask, the answer is no. But when the answer is yes, you are truly given a gift to connect in a very personal way. When you have created a portrait that touches your soul, the connection can last a lifetime.

Scenes of Daily Life

We often arrive at a destination with a vision in our head about what we want to photograph. We have consumed the brochures. We have researched several different itineraries and scoured the Internet comparing the itineraries to photographs of every destination. We arrive with a "shot list" of those "must-have" photographs we hope to replicate. But everything we see on tour can make a wonderful travel photograph if we take the time to notice.

OPPOSITE PAGE: São Goncalo dos Campos, Brazil
BELOW LEFT TO RIGHT: Tel Aviv, Israel; Jerusalem, Israel

Even in very touristy places, some of the most memorable photographs can be of the people we see around the tourist event or historic monument. Simple scenes of everyday life will help tell the story of your travel adventure. Walk slowly or stand alone in a quiet corner and watch as life passes by. Traveling is a wonderful chance to reconnect with the human spirit. When we are home, we rarely take time to witness simple scenes of everyday life. Our cities and neighborhoods are so familiar we have stopped seeing the people whose paths we cross as we go about our business and live our lives.

The more exotic the destination, the more strange and interesting life will seem. Even little things that go unnoticed by locals will catch your eye and show a different side of the experience. Children running in a park, people laughing at a café, commuters passing by on their way to work, or a young couple holding hands while walking in the rain can make for wonderful destination photographs.

Markets and bazaars are also great places to find colorful and lively scenes that reflect the culture of a community. Strange and unfamiliar foods, spices, clothing, jewelry, tourist trinkets, and lots of locals make for some of the best photo opportunities on tour. They can also be loud and intimidating. A great way of asking for portraits in a market is to purchase something first. My groups often buy rice and other staple foods in exchange for portraits and bring them as gifts to remote tribal communities. Win win!

All those who can read the sign will share in the irony…

Humor and Irony

Photographs have a natural ability to elicit an emotional response. Love, sorrow, anger, and happiness are fairly easy to recognize and usually connect with our shared experiences. While humor is also a fundamental human experience, what makes us laugh or what we find to be funny is different for each of us. Our cultural upbringing, age, and individual taste make humor difficult to define and even more difficult to explain. A joke told to one audience might not be funny at all or even understood by people of a different culture. But most of what makes us laugh has to do with our interactions with other people.

Photographers with an eye for the funny side of life can find humorous and ironic images where cultures overlap and when different elements in a photograph display a contradiction or incongruity. Fate, luck, karma, chance, and coincidence can sometimes be a photographer's strongest ally. Stumbling onto a pleasant surprise or making an unexpected discovery that inspires a chuckle is a happy accident that can lead to some fun and culturally interesting photographs.

A simple and easily discernible form of humor is irony. Tourists recognize irony when something is counter to what is expected, like when written language is contradicted by physical behavior. A photograph of a boy removing his shoes at the Taj Mahal in India is only funny and ironic because he is doing it in front of a large pile of shoes next to sign that reads, "Please do no take off your shoes here." All those who can read the sign will share in the irony, whether or not they find it to be funny.

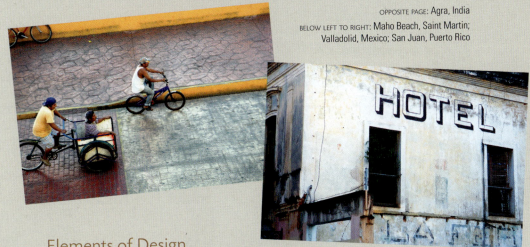

OPPOSITE PAGE: Agra, India
BELOW LEFT TO RIGHT: Maho Beach, Saint Martin; Valladolid, Mexico; San Juan, Puerto Rico

Elements of Design

The most memorable images are often those with a simple composition, an immediate impact, and which trigger an emotional response. They are often recognizable and relate to our own personal and cultural experiences. They require little analysis to extract meaning. The photographer has manipulated the elements of design to achieve a visual story that causes a viewer's response. To put it another way, a successful image isn't boring.

Line – The visual path that enables the eye to move within the photograph.

It can be explicit in the image like a line painted on a road, or implied by the borders and edges between elements and shapes.

Shape – An enclosed area defined by lines, edges, or contrast within the image. Circles, squares, triangles, and other shapes can be geometric (man made) or organic (formed by the arrangements of elements in the photograph).

Color – Hues with various intensities are perceived when light is reflected off an object back to the eye.

Texture – Surface qualities that translate into tactile illusions: rough or bumpy, smooth or reflective.

Tone/Value – Shading used to emphasize form. The relative lightness or darkness of an object emphasizes shape and the direction of a light source.

Form – In two-dimensional images, form is the perception of a three-dimensional object with length, width, and depth within a volume of space.

Space – The space taken up by objects (positive) or areas around or in between objects (negative). The interplay of spaces adds depth to a photograph through the use of perspective: foreground, middle ground, and background.

Environmental Portrait

The appeal of traveling to faraway lands is that, for a short time, we can escape our normal lives and experience the scenes, landscapes, and cultures of another people. Our senses are infused with a new set of stimuli as we see, smell, and hear the unfamiliar. These unfamiliar environments become the backgrounds for our travel photographs. While a great portrait of a face can reveal the soul of a person, a portrait that places the person in a location can tell us about how our subject lives and give context to the encounter. The environment becomes a significant element in the photographic narrative.

We are all in some kind of environment. It may be natural or artificial, but when we encounter people as travelers, we are in their home. Start with people you naturally encounter while traveling. Photographs of people in action, doing what they do, are often more relaxed than staged, formal portraits. Since the environment is an important part of the image, care must be taken to look into the background and notice how the subject is framed by their surroundings. While the background can add interest and context, it can also become a distraction. The environment shouldn't overpower the person.

What sets an environmental portrait apart from candid shots of everyday life is that the subject has agreed to be photographed and assumes a pose. If your subject was doing something before you approached them, start by having them continue the action. Much like the

OPPOSITE PAGE LEFT TO RIGHT: Kashgar, China; Lhasa, Tibet; Bagan, Myanmar
BELOW LEFT TO RIGHT: Kolkata, India; Roseau, Dominica; Cuzco, Peru

traditional headshot, the connection between the photographer and the subject provides the authenticity. If you have time and permission, move around the environment and try different things: with or without eye contact, smile or no smile, action or calm. You can control the mood you are trying to capture.

Most of all, if you have a willing subject, have fun. If you can make someone feel comfortable, both you and your subject will loosen up and your pictures will be more natural. You can't be shy and create successful portraits of strangers. All that is required to create great travel portraits is courage, empathy, understanding, creativity, and the curiosity to explore the human condition.

The World at Work

The many places we live and the many ways that we work are fascinating subjects for any curious photographer. For one person, going to work might mean putting on a business suit and taking public transportation to an inner-city office. For others, it might mean laboring from sun up to sun down tending to agricultural fields or selling fish in a local market. Photographs of people working can reveal the character of a culture or country and provide a glimpse of what life is like in different parts of the world.

Unlike other types of portraits and street scenes, people at work in a public place can usually be photographed candidly, and the photographer will go mostly unnoticed or at least will

Where People Gather **59**

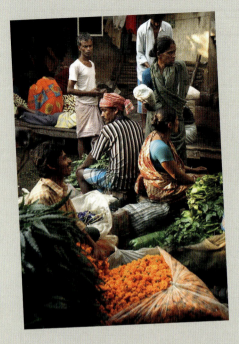

Principles of Design

Visual images are never just given to us, they are presented, and the form of that presentation is key to determining the ways in which the image succeeds in communicating and fascinating. Principles of design are different than elements of design. These principles relate to how the elements are organized in an image and how we read the image for meaning.

Emphasis is given to elements in the composition that direct the viewer's eye to important parts of the picture. Selective focus, framing, leading lines, and convergence create degrees of importance.

Balance is the perception of an equal distribution of visual weight in the image. A balanced image allows the viewer's eyes to roam around the entire piece. An unbalanced image will cause the viewer's gaze to be stuck on one element.

Visual Weight is the ability of elements within a two-dimensional picture to draw or repel the movement of the eye within the frame. Larger objects appear heavier than small objects. Different colors have different visual weight. Darker tones and colors carry more weight than lighter ones.

Contrast is the level of opposing qualities of elements next to each other in an image. The greater the contrast, the more visual interest an element or shape will have.

Unity is achieved when the individual elements work together for a balanced whole. The parts relate to each other in a logical progression rather than as a disorganized assortment of elements.

Movement adds excitement and tension to the work by directing the viewer's eye along a path through the image to a point of emphasis. If the subject isn't moving itself, movement can be created by line, shape, and color.

Rhythm is a lyrical quality that adds interest and movement achieved through the repetition or alternating progression of shapes, tones, or colors.

OPPOSITE PAGE: Kolkata, India
RIGHT: Chiang Rai, Thailand

be quickly forgotten as they tend to their business. Cooks, shopkeepers, street vendors, farmers, fishermen, rickshaw or taxi drivers, construction workers, dock workers, or even a local barber can make wonderful travel photographs.

Sometimes the easiest people to photograph on the job are directly related to the tourism industry, like the hotel or cruise ship staff, guides, or performers. Often tours will take tourists into shopping malls, restaurants, and bazaars, or provide opportunities to go behind the scenes in manufacturing facilities and workshops. The idea is to concentrate on telling the story of what your subject does with his or her life. This is often accomplished with a wide shot that shows the environment, but foreground elements and props can provide clues to the job or location.

Like environmental portraits, capturing people in a setting that is comfortable and familiar to them can make for more relaxed and natural photographs. Most occupations also have some unique or characteristic tools, clothing, uniforms, hats or helmets, or other distinctive elements that can add interest to the image story. Facial expressions can provide action to the scene, and movement allows for you to capture a decisive moment. Since this type of people photography is less intrusive than approaching someone for a portrait, they will usually not mind being watched or photographed. But again, don't be sneaky when shooting candid shots of people. If you are noticed, be polite and smile.

A Compelling Face

When we travel, we are naturally drawn to faces that seem to capture the essence of a place. A compelling face can carry the story of an entire culture. Indigenous people dressed in their traditional clothing are irresistible for photographers. But they have also seen postcards and tour books with their tribal likenesses for sale or used for tourism marketing. They know

professional photographers are making money off of their images, which makes it difficult for anyone to photograph them without negotiating compensation. The resulting photographs are usually disappointing snapshots.

The problem facing a tourist photographer is how to find and capture authenticity that is hidden below the staged event, the humanity that is revealed in a fleeting glance, a genuine smile, or a moment of quiet reflection. To find something "real" in a contrived situation, you need to reach across cultural barriers to make an authentic human connection. When our tourist interactions are peer-to-peer and mutually rewarding, we don't just look and photograph, we learn from each other.

Since most organized tours will have a guide who speaks the local language, approaching an interesting older woman on the streets or in a market can be much easier. You might not get her permission to make a portrait, but looking like a tourist can be disarming and you might create a nice travel memory through conversation. I have often been asked why I want to take a picture. My favorite answer for my translator to share is, "Tell her I think she is beautiful and when I return home, I want to remember that we met today."

Human Connections

As a part of the human condition, we instinctively read faces to determine if a person is a friend or a threat. Are they smiling? Are they calm, agitated, upset, or excited? Is the gaze confrontational, sincere, seductive, or uncomfortable? We make these judgments almost instantaneously. We sense the emotion of the other person and react intuitively and empathetically. A photograph also triggers these emotional responses. In a simple portrait we can sense sadness and fear or joy and happiness. To read these emotions, we often look to the eyes.

For a photographer, eye contact is an important consideration. If the subject is looking directly into the camera when photographed, it is almost impossible for a viewer not to look at them. They are staring at us, demanding a reaction. Without eye contact, the mood of the photograph changes, often dramatically. The intimacy of the gaze is reduced to a remote appreciation. Without the confrontation of eye contact, the viewer becomes an observer of the scene and is released to explore it at a comfortable distance.

The direction in which the subject is looking can also have a large impact on the mood and emotional intensity of a photograph. The powerful connection we have through our eyes is also the reason that we will follow the gaze of a subject in a photograph. We are fascinated by what other people are looking at. The gaze becomes as powerful as a leading line. If the subject is looking at something within the frame, a second point of interest will be created. A subject looking out of the frame can create a feeling of tension or provide a sense of candidness to a portrait. If it is mystery you are going for, moving images are often found in a passing glance or a moment of relaxed contemplation.

FIELD NOTES

Alone Time in Kolkata

On my first visit to India, I had the opportunity to walk the streets of Kolkata almost exactly ten years after the death of Mother Teresa. For nearly fifty years, Mother Teresa devoted herself to helping the poorest of the poor in India's third most populated metropolitan area. Even today, it is estimated that 10 percent of Kolkata's 45 million residents are homeless and living on the streets or in shanties. Conservative estimates put the number of homeless children around 100,000.

The narrow lanes in the northern part of the city are hot, dirty, and filled with streaming crowds of people, rickshaws, and animals. As a photographer walking alone in this unfamiliar city, I clearly didn't blend into the local community. Unlike other parts of the world, where chronic poverty has bred desperation and anger, the people I met as I wandered the serpentine alleyways were curious, kind, and engaging. I was most certainly noticed, but the gritty backstreets and oldest neighborhoods

of Kolkata aren't flush with tourists, which can often bring out hawkers and predators. In the same Kolkata neighborhoods where Mother Teresa spread love and kindness, I was free to roam.

As I walked away from the main arterial roads, I found myself on quiet streets where dark narrow lanes were draped with laundry, and children ran and played while skilled clay sculptors were busy making Hindu idols. I was in the Kumartuli cultural precinct of Kolkata, known as the "alley of potters." Everywhere along the awning-covered streets and behind the doors of small workshops, clay figures were being molded in mud.

I stopped several times to meet and photograph the artisans at work. They were indifferent to my presence, but I could also feel their sense of pride that a foreigner was taking an interest in their art. During my short walk, I was followed by a group of young boys, I prodded a shy older woman to let me take her picture, and I met a beautiful little girl sitting quietly near the family workshop. I took a couple pictures of her from a distance before noticing her father watching in the background. I stopped, smiled at him, and pointed to my camera. With a gentle nod he gave me permission to come closer and to meet and photograph his little girl.

GYPSIES
GODS & DROMEDARIES

From a distance, the hundreds of tents in endless rows on the outskirts of Pushkar looked like the military encampment of a besieging army. I hopped off my camel cart to walk the sandy corridors between tents where thousands of desert nomads were welcoming a new day. The barren dunes were coming to life with the traders, gypsies, and pilgrims who descend on this sleepy lakeside city every year from all over India.

Countless camels kicked up the desert sands, raising a cloud of suffocating dust under the heat of the rising sun, while cattle and goat herders watered their animals at large communal troughs. Women in bright saris collected camel dung, patting it with bare hands into pancakes to be used as fuel for cooking. In the distance a group of men huddled around a smoky campfire as children rubbed sleep from their eyes with their tiny fists.

Through the gritty haze, I caught the attention of a woman who approached me slowly but confidently. Her long red scarf flowed and danced along the sand behind her as she walked. We made eye contact, and I stopped to await her advance. In anticipation of the request I knew would soon follow, I casually reached into my pocket to see if I still had a few small bills tucked away. She was bangled and bejeweled, with an exotic beauty unlike any beggar I have ever encountered. Her captivating gaze was

intensified by a few precise strokes of black eyeliner. Her hair was restrained with matching red pins, and her nose was pierced and strung with a cherished adornment. In a soft, heavily accented voice, she smiled at me and whispered, "Photo?"

It was no doubt one of the few English words she knew, but she was clearly aware of her striking beauty and its value as a photographic souvenir, and she fully expected to be compensated for the snapshots. I rarely pay for photographs of people I meet through a chance encounter on the streets of a foreign land, but I found her graceful self-confidence and exotic charm irresistible. As I continued toward the heart of the city, she was the first and most interesting of the onslaught of beggars, hawkers, and performers that approached me, each looking to begin their day by earning or otherwise acquiring a few easy rupees from the first foreigner who crossed their path.

I eventually made my way through the persistent young men vigorously pursuing a sale of postcards, beads, trinkets, or toys to the winding streets of the Sadar Bazaar and the markets near the Brahma Temple. Storefront shops selling jewelry, handbags, fabrics, and carpets captured the attention of women, while fruits and vegetables were sold in ad hoc markets. Hundreds of brightly dressed pilgrims formed a long line leading up the marble steps to the temple. I was consumed by the riot of color and fascinating mix of aggressive commerce and uninhibited piety that defines the Pushkar experience.

The Brahma Temple is the most famous and most significant of Pushkar's four hundred temples and one of the few found anywhere in the world dedicated to Lord Brahma, the creator of the universe. Easily identified by its distinctive 690-foot-high (210 m) red spire, the temple is one of the most sacred pilgrimage destinations for Hindus. For many, pilgrimage is also their preferred form of tourism. They flock to the ghats and temples of cities like Pushkar and Varanasi, traveling with their families and community groups for an enjoyable and spiritual vacation. Festivals and fairs often develop during auspicious times of the year, adding a lively atmosphere and holiday spirit to the lure of these important sites.

THERE ARE MANY LEGENDS associated with the origin of Pushkar, but they all involve Lord Brahma. Lord Brahma is one god of the holy Hindu trinity of gods known as Trimurtis. They are Brahma, Vishnu, and Shiva: the creator, the preserver, and the destroyer. As the legend goes, Pushkar Lake was created when a lotus petal (*pushpa*) fell from the hand (*kar*) of Brahma and dropped into the valley surrounded by the Aravali Hills. When Brahma came down to earth, he named the place where the flower landed Pushkar, and water soon sprouted from the desert to form the lake.

On the day of the autumn full moon, this small city of whitewashed buildings along the banks of a miraculous lake becomes the holiest

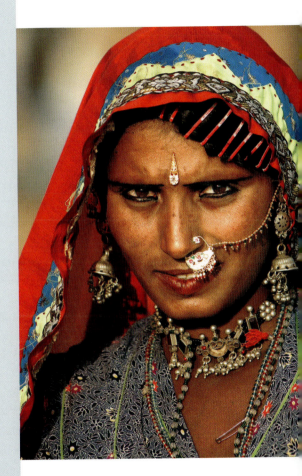

place on earth for Hindus. It is also believed that during this extraordinary period of time, all of the 330 million Hindu gods join bathers in Pushkar Lake in celebration of the creator. Pilgrims from all over India come by train, bus, and camel cart to bathe with the gods. The permanent population of just fifteen thousand residents is overwhelmed by tens of thousands of devout Hindus who come to Pushkar looking for enlightenment and salvation at the edge of the holy lake. But they also come to shop the local markets and to be entertained by camel races, amusement rides, and tribal performers from the deserts of Rajasthan at the largest fair of its kind anywhere in the world.

The first five days of the Pushkar Camel Fair are a time of carnival and camel, before the focus shifts to the religious festival of Kartik Purnima. In this tale of two cities, the peaceful pilgrim town explodes into a spectacle of local culture, layered and intertwined with myth, history, and spirituality, resulting in a bewildering bazaar of gypsies, gods, and dromedaries. There are snake charmers, whose hypnotic music entices cobras to rise out of wicker baskets and dance, elaborately dressed street performers, ash-covered Sadhus lost in a spiritual trance, and six-legged cows, whose owners highlight their deformities to elicit money from the curious. Most of all, there are tribal women in their colorful saris and thousands of amazing faces that reflect the long and fascinating history of an ancient culture that continues to live in the heart and soul of Rajasthan.

FOR POOR AND MARGINAL COMMUNITIES like the seminomadic caste called Raika, the camel is the foundation of their livelihood. In the desert, the docile creature is used as a beast of burden and mode of transportation; its dung is used for fuel, its milk is used for food, and upon its death, its hide is used for leather. The Raika are the historic camel breeders of Rajasthan and one of an estimated five hundred nomadic groups in India. For centuries the camel was their currency and this annual fair was important family business. Owning camels was once a sign of wealth and status.

Their tribal creation story claims that their ancestors were brought into existence by Lord Shiva in order to tend for the first camel, which was created for the amusement of the Hindu goddess Parvati. The Raika have historically taken this divine charge seriously, developing a unique bond with their camels. Their culture is also a product of the environment in Rajasthan, an arid state in northwest India where wealthy maharajahs built opulent palaces and spectacular fortresses. For thousands of years, the camel served many purposes including being the preferred ride of a wartime cavalry, which continues to patrol the remote desert border with Pakistan.

Increasing pressure on pasture lands and the increasing ability of farmers to afford modern equipment are turning younger generations of Raika away from their hereditary occupation in search of menial work in India's major cities. As a result, the "ship of the desert" is now sold for slaughter, and the future of this noble trade is in doubt. As recently as fifteen years earlier, selling camels for meat and leather at the Pushkar Camel Fair would have been unheard of, but the camel business is becoming more difficult and less profitable. Fewer young camels are bought and sold, and the Raika who are still involved in animal husbandry also raise sheep and goats. Times are changing for the camel breeders of antiquity.

It is estimated that 7 percent of the population of India is made up of nomadic tribal groups. The remote desert state of Rajasthan has more than double the national average, and they have a long history. A thousand years ago, a group of nomads left the Thar Desert, traveling through the Middle East and reaching Europe late in the thirteenth century. Eventually, this migration spread across the entire world. They are the Romani and they have been called "gypsies" in one language or another in nations on every continent. It is a word that has come to define the fictional way of life of a traveling population that uses their wits and talents to earn a living, often outside the boundaries of the law.

But the realities of so-called gypsies are always more complex. In modern times, these descendants of early Rajput clans from western India have been persecuted and discriminated against everywhere they have called home. Their brethren who remained in Rajasthan have not fared much better, sharing the bad reputation and suspicion that follow the world's wandering tribes.

Gypsies, Gods, and Dromedaries 71

While India continues to fight the remnants of the caste system, it remains a stratified society that has little use for the people who continue to wander the subcontinent. India's nomads, gypsies, and traveling craftsmen who serviced and performed for princes and maharajas now largely depend on begging to survive or literally singing and dancing for their supper. Today, the once-considered honorable castes of fortunetellers, healers, jugglers, snake charmers, dancers, and storytellers have settled near tourist cities like Pushkar and gather at the many seasonal festivals, entertaining pilgrims and tourists for small donations.

THE BEAUTIFUL AND EXOTIC WOMAN I met and photographed in the fairgrounds belongs to one of the lowest castes in India, the Kalbeliya. They are known as the snake charmer caste. Their women are skilled dancers, beggars, and singers who follow fairs and festivals, performing traditional songs and dance, many of which have gone viral, entertaining curious YouTube travelers who will never find their way to Pushkar.

During the Pushkar Camel Fair, these service castes of India's western desert mingle with higher-caste pilgrims who have come to visit Pushkar's ghats and temples during this auspicious time. The intensity created by the crush of two hundred thousand people and well over twenty thousand camels is palpable for foreigners who are hounded for a tiny token of their wealth. But the Pushkar Camel Festival is also an opportunity for tourists to catch a glimpse of India's cultural past, a thrilling immersion into the lives of marginalized people who live at the fringes of a high-speed, high-tech, modern economy.

The fair is a chance for Rajasthan's nomadic tribes to meet old friends and enjoy a welcomed break from the harshness of their daily lives. It is a chance for families to indulge in music, dances, games, and shopping after the business of the day is completed. The annual gathering at Pushkar is not a tourist extravaganza. It is their party, their fair, and their festival. Smiles and laughter add to the air of festivity at the camel races and beauty contests. Girlish giggles suggest the lightness of the moment as scores of young women wait in line at the Ferris wheels that tower above the desert horizon.

OPPOSITE PAGE: Sulamani Temple, Bagan, Myanmar

Chapter 4
Spiritual Worlds and Sacred Places

"Often while traveling with a camera, we arrive just as the sun slips over the horizon of a moment, too late to expose film, only time enough to expose our hearts."
—Minor White

Religious tourism has existed since the first pilgrimages of antiquity. Sacred sites are special places where the physical world meets the spiritual world for literally billions of people. The religious traditions of other countries and cultures are a source of fascination and curiosity. Some of the most spectacular sights in the world are the buildings, shrines, and sculptures that are central to the history of a faith or religion.

Today, holy places are almost always woven into tourist itineraries. Many are also places of pilgrimage, which can produce a nervous tension when the two groups of travelers unavoidably intermingle. Religious pilgrims travel on a sacred journey to affirm their faith or make a transformative connection to their god. Tourists visit holy places as observers and photographers of the human condition, drawn to the passion of the faithful in search of insight and understanding.

As tourists, we may never truly understand the strongly held beliefs of others, but if we can suspend judgment for an hour, or a day, or a week, visiting the most spiritual places on earth can be among the most profound and intense reflections of the human spirit that we will ever witness. You don't have to be a believer or share the faith to recognize the magnificence of European cathedrals and Buddhist temples, appreciate the complexities of Hindu rituals, be touched by passionate tears at the Western Wall, or be moved by the distant call to prayer carried on the morning breeze from unseen loudspeakers.

Cultural Etiquette

While cultural sensitivity is important wherever you travel, it is even more so when visiting religious sites. The details of proper global comportment and etiquette are infinite. It is impossible to know the complexities and nuances of every religion and culture, but some understanding of local customs and protocol will certainly enhance your experience and help you avoid a possibly offensive or embarrassing situation.

When we go on tour in a foreign land, we often go with preconceptions and expectations. We have often spent a lot of money and are determined to capture new and exciting wonders in our photographs. Every photographer wants to produce the beautiful shot that will reveal the spiritual significance of a place, but the worst thing you can do is to try to be surreptitious. You will be noticed. Tourists with cameras at religious events or holy places will often be viewed with mistrust. Spiritual sites magnify already significant cultural differences.

There are certainly many things to be aware of when photographing culturally sensitive places, but, in famous tourist spots, the rules are often posted and easy to follow. The most important thing to remember is "No" means "No." You are visiting a spiritual place that is attempting to preserve its original purpose before it became a tourist attraction. At some

OPPOSITE PAGE LEFT TO RIGHT: Thyangboche, Nepal; Id Kah Mosque, Kashgar, China
RIGHT: Hagia Sofia, Istanbul, Turkey

places photography is simply not allowed or a flash and tripod are restricted. Respect that the site you are visiting is very important to a lot of people and try to navigate through our increasingly accessible world with sensitivity.

Houses of Worship

Some of the world's oldest and most beautiful buildings are places of worship that have been built to impress. They are glorious monuments of faith set aside as holy houses dedicated to the worship of gods and goddesses. Temples, churches, mosques, and synagogues have been constructed for centuries as sacred spaces to perform acts of devotion. Within their walls exists a living history that has evolved over time to reflect the beliefs and aesthetic choices of a culture.

By their very nature, places of worship in city centers are often very large buildings, crowded with both worshipers and tourists. Crafted with the intricate tile and stonework of artisans and adorned with gold, glass, and precious stones, they are ornate and photogenic architectural structures. Sacred architecture has influenced and reflected every architectural style in world history. Spires, bell towers, flying buttresses, massive domes, stupas, and minarets grace the skylines and flank the rivers of the world's great cities.

Artificial Light

One of the truly wonderful aspects of digital photography is how easy it is to compensate for different light sources. While most travel photography is with natural light, artificial light is sometimes unavoidable. Each light source, from incandescent bulbs to fluorescent and mercury vapor, has a different color temperature. In the old days of using film, that meant attaching color compensation filters in front of the lens. Today, it is a matter of selecting the appropriate white balance.

Tourists will typically encounter artificial light sources at night or while shooting indoors. Setting for automatic white balance will adequately adjust for most variations of color temperature, but where two or more different types of light are present, the photographer must make a choice. This is most often encountered where a portion of the scene is lit by window light while other areas are lit by incandescent bulbs that give off an orange glow, or by fluorescent lights that have a green cast.

It isn't always necessary to produce a perfectly clean image with corrected white balance. Sometimes the warm glow of tungsten bulbs can add a certain ambience, mood, or atmosphere that is pleasing to the overall effect of the photograph. Street scenes and cityscapes take on a very different visual feel when the lights come on. The neon glow of signs and billboards, the interior lights of buildings and restaurants, and the streaming lights of cars and taxis are wonderful subjects to explore after dark.

From the open courtyards of early mosques to the dark stained-glass light inside Christian cathedrals, places of worship can be challenging subjects to photograph. It is often difficult to capture the full façade or illustrate the massive expanse of a poorly illuminated interior. As tourists, we rarely get lucky enough to visit when the light is perfect. For instance, visiting a west-facing building in the morning will place the front façade into featureless shadow. Often, after attempting to capture the grandeur of a structure, I have concentrated my time on finding interesting details and the religious motifs that are endemic to sacred architecture.

The beauty and architectural style of a building can often be discovered in the smallest of details. Fill your frame with the archway of a door or window. Capture the warm light of afternoon as it exposes the subtle textures of mosaic tiles, or use a long lens to compress repeating details like arches and rooftops to produce interesting patterns.

Tourists can often photograph the exteriors with complete freedom, but shooting inside is often much more difficult, both culturally and photographically. The shadowed arches and dark vaulted spaces, poorly illuminated by small incandescent bulbs and filtered window light,

OPPOSITE PAGE: Notre-Dame Cathedral, Paris, France
BELOW: Chiang Mai, Thailand

require special attention. Since flash and tripods are almost always forbidden, brace yourself against a pillar or wall, or use a pew or rail to steady your camera. Look for candlelit corners and areas illuminated by a single light source.

Worshipers, Offerings, and Rituals

When visiting a country or culture where religion is a visible part of everyday life, pictures of people praying, meditating, and making offerings are as irresistible as the spectacles of indigenous tribal cultures. Sacred rituals performed by the devout dressed in religious clothing that has special significance to a particular faith or group can make powerful images that communicate depth and spirituality. They just need to be approached with care.

The intent isn't simply to not disrupt the experience. In many religious cultures an aggressive tourist photographer can face a sharp response for his or her insensitivity. There is a difference between having permission to photograph a scene and doing it with understanding. In most times and in most places, you should never come between a worshiper and what they are praying to. Even though many religious activities occur in public spaces, we all have a personal boundary that should be respected. There is a time and a place for an intimate portrait, but approaching worshipers praying isn't one of them. This is a good time to use a longer lens and work from the sidelines.

It is, however, quite easy to photograph public rituals and festivals. Most participants understand that they are in a public space, at a public event, or engaging in a public celebration. Even the seemingly simple act of lighting a candle or making an offering of flowers can yield a wonderfully expressive image that will contribute subtle religious overtones to the story of your destination.

Music, dance, food, costumes, ritual bathing, and group performances often accompany religious celebrations and are performed all over the world. Likewise, bathers along the banks of the Ganges or Orthodox Jews at the Western Wall (except on the Shabbat when photographs at the wall are prohibited) know that they are the subjects of curious tourists and are often so engaged with their own interests that they barely notice a discreet photographer.

BELOW: Bagan, Myanmar
OPPOSITE PAGE LEFT TO RIGHT: Gongkar Monastery, Tibet; Phuket, Thailand

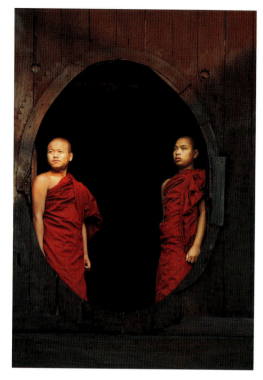

Monks and Nuns

Throughout Asia, tourists encounter Buddhist monks and nuns with regularity. Sometimes, the encounters are in a structured setting like a temple or monastery, or when collecting alms. Other times, they are waiting at a bus stop on a city street or riding a water taxi on a river. Obviously, what makes monks and nuns such wonderful photographic subjects is the uniqueness of their dress and how their very presence provides a sense of place and a touch of spiritual mystery.

Many temples don't allow photographs of sacred objects, but most monks and nuns are accommodating to tourist photographers if approached with respect. They certainly understand that they are an important part of the tourist experience and have opened their places of worship to the tourist gaze. As you might expect, each country, religious order, sect, and temple will have different rules to photograph inside their place of worship. Don't be surprised if there is a small photography fee or that you will be required to remove your shoes or cover your shoulders or legs before entering.

Just like any other portrait, the challenge isn't simply to capture the likeness of a monk or a nun in a photographic image, it is in attempting to capture what isn't visible—their sense of spirituality, which can reveal the heart and soul of a culture. Their rituals have meaning. Their routines and behaviors have been developed

Fill Flash

I am not a big fan of flash photography. I much prefer to work around the natural lighting conditions on location, but sometimes using a flash is necessary. A great use for flash is also for outdoor portraits in bright sunlight. Harsh light creates deep, distracting shadows, dark eye sockets, and unattractive shadows under the nose and lips. A gentle fill-flash can add details, open shadows, and add a little reflection in the eye, known as a catch-light, without changing the lighting characteristic of the scene.

Fill-flash looks most natural when it is a stop or two darker than the natural light. If the flash is too strong, the portrait will look like you used a flash and be less natural. Fill-flash should barely be noticed and never create background shadows. There are multiple diffusers on the market that will soften the light of your flash. Today, most built-in and dedicated flash units have a mode just for fill-flash or allow you to control the brightness of the fill, making exposure almost foolproof.

Spirtual Worlds and Sacred Places

OPPOSITE PAGE LEFT TO RIGHT: Khumbu Region, Nepal; Wat Mahathat, Ayutthaya, Thailand

over centuries. They have devoted their lives to the pursuit of something profound. As tourists we can't possibly know the extent of their sacrifice, but our photography is more than a simple record of our chance encounters. We make images based on our own perceptions of a shared humanity, and a great portrait is also a reflection of our empathy and understanding.

Symbols and Sacred Objects

Another interesting way to portray a religious travel experience is by shooting the things that surround the spiritual practice. All religions have symbols, regalia, and sacred objects that represent the faith or are used in the rituals of worship. Just as architectural details complete the story of houses of worship, photographs of prayer wheels, bells, bowls, instruments, flags, statues, candles, scriptures, clothing, beads, icons, and idols can communicate religious and cultural significance.

For a visual storyteller, objects and symbols represent the concept of faith and can reveal many subtle aspects of different religions and the relationships people have with them. Throughout history, ceremonial and ritualistic objects have been used to bring us comfort, gain merit, or communicate and connect with a world beyond our understanding. Practitioners often carry special objects in their pockets, hang the symbols of their faith around their neck, and display representations in the attempt to see what is unseen.

Besides the obvious, like the Christian cross or Star of David of Judaism, our travels are often infused with objects that have sacred symbolic meanings. The Buddha image in its many forms has become one of the most popular representations in Buddhism, and it is quite common to find a small shrine on the dashboard of your taxi in India in tribute to any number of Hindu gods. In many cultures, the objects of daily life are both utilitarian and representative. Jewelry or a single article of clothing, like the veiled face of a woman or the skull cap of a man, can instantly communicate cultural, religious, and geographic information.

It is impossible to travel into Buddhist regions of the Himalaya and not notice the colorful prayer flags draped and strung along mountain ridges and auspicious places, or see the mantra of *"om mani padme hum"* painted or carved into collections of stones. When strings of colored prayer flags are placed high in the mountains, the symbols and sacred text printed on them are carried on the wind to spread good will and compassion for the benefit of the world. How can that not be a good thing?

We make images based on our own perceptions of a shared humanity, and a great portrait is also a reflection of our empathy and understanding.

Spiritual Worlds and Sacred Places

FIELD NOTES

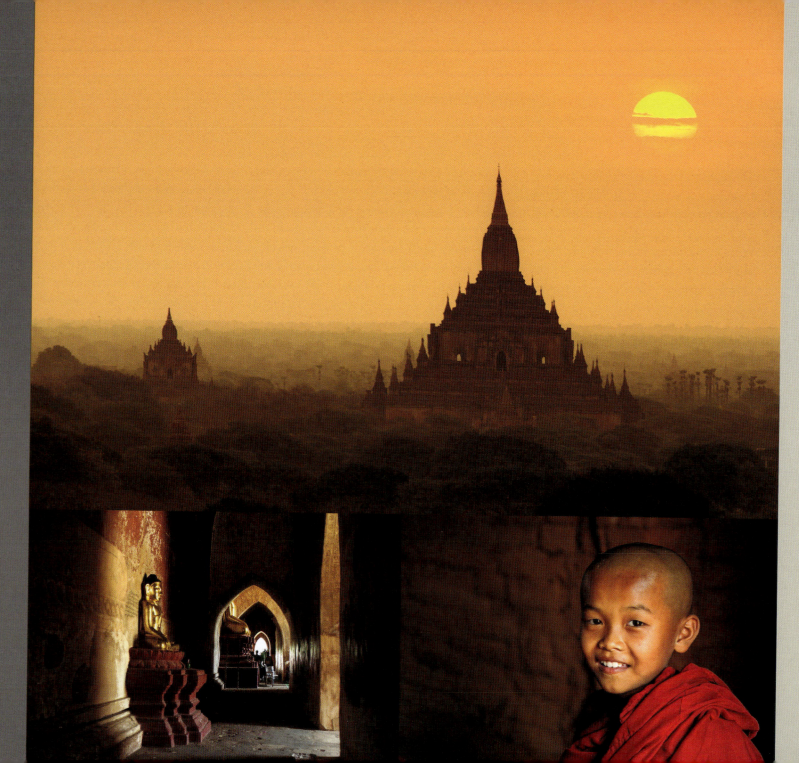

Sunrise Over Bagan

I motored north out of New Bagan on a rented electric bike, chasing the small pool of light cast by my headlamp on the street in front of me. I was one of the first to arrive at Shwesandaw Pagoda. I slowly and carefully climbed the steep steps, barefoot in the darkness, as countless thousands had before. The distant sound of a deep melodic voice reciting prayers in an unfamiliar language added a lyrical soundtrack to my vision of a hauntingly beautiful landscape partially shrouded in the predawn haze.

Shwesandaw is a white pyramid-style pagoda with five terraces surrounding a circular stupa; it is also one of the few architectural icons of Bagan that tourists can climb. I waited on the uppermost terrace with my camera mounted on a tripod, trained to the east in anticipation of a magical sunrise reveal. As the minutes passed, the spectacular Sulamani temple formed a striking silhouette against the brightening sky, while other temples and pagodas could be seen as small shapely shadows nestled between the trees on the dusty valley floor. The reddish-brown hue of ancient brickwork was soon bathed in the warm glow of the rising sun.

It is estimated that more than ten thousand Buddhist temples, pagodas, and monasteries were once scattered across the plains of central Myanmar (Burma) along a bend in the Ayeyarwady River. Between the tenth and thirteenth centuries, Bagan was the capital of a vast kingdom. Despite nearly eight hundred years of neglect, erosion, and the devastating effects of earthquakes, the temple-studded landscape has become one of the world's great religious and historic sites. The beautiful photogenic structures hint at the grandeur of the past. Today, only a handful of the two thousand remaining and largely rebuilt and renovated religious sites continue to be active places of worship.

Nearly 90 percent of Myanmar's population is Buddhist, and every man is expected to don monastic robes for a brief period in their lives, usually between the ages of seven and twelve. Throughout Myanmar, Buddhist monks are a part of the landscape of daily life. Every morning at dawn, they can be seen walking the streets around their monasteries collecting alms. The act of giving alms, as food or money, is a common practice among Buddhists and is a symbolic connection to the spiritual world that shows humbleness and respect. During the summer months of March, April, and May, novice monks tour the impressive Buddha images of Bagan as they carry forward the traditions and historic spirituality that is the religious soul of Myanmar.

Until recently, the people of Myanmar and the stories of its culture have largely been ignored by the outside world. Run by an often-brutal military regime since 1962, the country was essentially cut off from tourism for fifty years. Following the first elections in two decades, a process of reform was initiated in 2010, and a new wave of western tourists began to join pilgrims, monks, and nuns in this once isolated country to marvel at the remnants of the grand imperial capital in Bagan. As curious travelers, we are drawn to places of relative isolation to witness a culture lightly influenced by outside forces. In Bagan, tourists from around the world are coming to witness the magical sunrise and search for something spiritual in the shadows of the ancient city.

FIELD NOTES

A Holy City in a Holy Land

As I approached the Western Wall of the Second Temple in Jerusalem, I felt a rush of adrenaline much like I felt when I entered the forecourt of the Jokang Temple in Tibet, walked down the ghats to the Ganges River in Varanasi, or witnessed morning prayers at the five-hundred-year-old Id Kah Mosque on the Muslim Day of Sacrifice in the fabled city of Kashgar. I was once again entering a sacred place where true believers display their devotion to the divine. With each step I made, I became more anxious about my visit to their holy site and how I would be received as I started taking pictures.

An eclectic stream of pilgrims, worshipers, and tourists made their way up and down the narrow, sloping corridor leading to the famous prayer section of the celebrated wall. Our group was given just twenty minutes before we were instructed to meet back in the large, open space of the plaza. I passed several men sitting in white plastic chairs reading scriptures

before taking a moment to lay my hands on the ancient stones, hoping that just maybe my simple touch would help me comprehend its holiness.

Several other tourists around me were taking pictures, so I slowly raised my camera to my eye. Since my time was short, I concentrated my attention on a group of Jewish men dressed in traditional orthodox clothing. I respectfully moved in and around trying not to invade their space, often pausing for just a moment to appreciate the spiritual atmosphere. After overstaying my welcome, I circled around and made my way back to the plaza with a mild sense of relief. The mood was much more relaxed just a short distance away from the wall as people talked and gathered.

The Western Wall refers to a retaining wall built by Herod the Great around 19 BCE to expand the footprint of the Temple Mount, which was destroyed in 70 CE by the Roman Empire following a Jewish revolt. But like all sacred sites, mere history doesn't explain the nature of its biblical significance. Human beings ascribe spiritual importance to places and objects that are believed to have a connection to their god. For thousands of years, Temple Mount was coveted and conquered for its spiritual and historic connections to the god of Abraham.

Temple Mount is located on Mount Moriah, built over the Foundation Stone, which, according to the sages of the Talmud, is where the world was created. It is the location of Solomon's temple where the Ark of the Covenant was kept and considered the "Holy of Holies" by the followers of Judaism. A bedrock outcropping now covered by the magnificent Dome of the Rock is where God ordered Abraham to bind his son Isaac for sacrifice. It is from this same rock that Muslims believe the prophet Muhammad ascended for a nightlong journey to heaven to receive the order of daily prayer for Islam. Today, it remains one of the most contentious fourteen hectares (thirty-five acres) in the world.

The history of Jerusalem has been stacked layer upon layer. The present is defined by the meaning and symbolism of the past. It is a place where politics and religion are forever intertwined and followers of the three monotheistic religions of Abraham are bound together. But amidst the holy sites and religious fervor, daily life persists in the four quarters of the Old City. Children play in the courtyards, souks crowd the dark, narrow alleyways, and shops and restaurants service tourists and pilgrims alike as they walk in the footsteps of Jesus toward the site of his crucifixion. Regardless of your faith or belief, it is impossible to walk these cobblestone streets of antiquity and deny that something important has happened here, or maybe…many important somethings.

The Sacred City of Shiva

It was only my first full day in India, but I was already beginning to appreciate the beauty and rhythm nestled amidst the seeming chaos that surrounded me. As the last bit of daylight surrendered to eerie pockets of neon illumination, I mounted a cycle-rickshaw near my hotel and was quickly swept through a narrow, meandering maze of tiny alleyways. Cars, rickshaws, scooters, bicycles, pedestrians, and sacred cows all competed for space in a disorderly ballet. Women dressed in saris created a colorful mosaic to accompany the cacophonous blare of honking horns that together turned the crowded streets into a noisy, swirling sea of humanity flowing toward the holy River Ganges.

After weaving my way through the growing crowd of pilgrims, tourists, beggars, hawkers, and homeless to the famous ghats along the river, I boarded an old wooden boat with several other curious foreigners. We were each handed a small candle packaged in a paper cup with orange marigold flowers to present as an offering to the river. Slowly, our two young boatmen maneuvered us forward until we reached an area where a dozen fires burned brightly in the blackness, their reflections dancing gently on the waves. As we neared the cremation ghat, Manikarnika, we joined several other boats filled with people silently witnessing a thousand-year-old drama unfolding before us. The only movement interrupting the respectful stillness was a young British couple carefully placing their fragile flames on the dark river in hopes that the gods might receive their prayers.

We didn't get close enough to see detail in the flames, but the unspoken reality of what was burning in the distance left us without words as our boatmen turned back toward the bright lights of the central ghats. While it is obvious that death is the most unavoidable of all human realities, it is welcomed in Varanasi without the fear or trepidation that can be so disturbing to Western sensibilities. Death is also an unavoidable part of the Varanasi experience. There are few places on earth where life and death are so easily embraced as two parts of a single whole, and tourists are confronted with an almost constant overlap of the physical and spiritual worlds. It is impossible to remain untouched by the atmosphere of devotion that defines Varanasi.

Before I had time to fully comprehend the unfamiliar sights and sounds, we found ourselves back at Dashashwamedh ghat where a mass of faithful were gathered for the nightly Aarti ceremony. A Hindu priest raised and lowered a glowing offering of open flames as the sounds of bells, chanting, and hypnotic song washed over us from unseen loudspeakers. As I steadied my camera to capture the spectacle, I felt completely overwhelmed by an intoxicating mix of adrenaline and jet lag. Nothing in my travels had prepared me for the intensity I was experiencing or the utterly bizarre collection of people that had somehow found their way to this particular place on this particular day.

For thousands of years, India's Hindus have been making the pilgrimage to Varanasi to be seen by the gods and to purify their souls in her holy waters. Also known as Benaras and Kashi (the City of Light) it is considered to be among the oldest living cities of the world. According to legend, the Hindu deity, Lord Shiva, founded the city around five thousand years ago. He is called Mahadev, the greatest of the gods, the one whom the gods themselves worship, and is thought by many to still live here, walking the streets of Varanasi in disguise. For Hindu faithful, Varanasi is the most sacred place on earth and the River Ganges, the holiest river. To bathe in its waters is said to lead one on a path to *moksha* (liberation). To die within sight of it is to be blessed and to be cremated and have your ashes scattered in the river is the final salvation in the endless cycle of birth and rebirth that is at the heart of Hindu philosophy.

People from all over India come to live out their lives in Varanasi. But it is not the physical

act of dying in Varanasi that liberates an individual from the cycle of endless births; it is the wisdom delivered by Shiva at the moment of death that releases the soul from suffering. It is Shiva himself who whispers the secret of Om, the verbal encapsulation of the "Supreme Reality," into the ears of the dying. This ultimate revelation of god, delivered by god, happens only in Varanasi where the sacred city, the home to Shiva, and the River Ganges form a triple blessing found nowhere else on earth.

The modern city of Varanasi is a city of poverty and wealth, joy and suffering, life and death. It is also home to one million residents who have built houses, schools, parks, cyber cafes, businesses, and luxury hotels among the temples, markets, mosques, and ashrams of antiquity. Just south of the city, the Benares Hindu University is a center of Sanskrit learning and Hindu philosophy that has been attracting students and scholars since the early 1900s.

For Buddhists throughout the world, nearby Sarnath is as sacred as Varanasi is to Hindus. The fifth century Dhamekh Stupa is said to have been built on the site where the enlightened Siddhartha Gautama, who came to be called Buddha, delivered his first sermon to five ascetics in 500 BCE. But by the time Buddha shared his Four Noble Truths at Deer Park, just six miles (10 km) northeast of Varanasi, the city was already a sacred gathering place and vibrant commercial center renowned for its weavers and spectacular brocades. Today, visitors still shop in the markets and fine textile shops for cotton weaves, saris, and scarves.

While Varanasi increasingly takes on modern textures, the city is largely an eighteenth century creation with a thirteenth century infrastructure. By the late 1700s, the holy city came under British administration and was substantially rebuilt through the patronage of the maharajas and India's princely states after a long period of neglect under Mughal dominance. Many of the city's most important temples and ghats date from this era, but the Varanasi we now visit was built in stages. Over hundreds of years, talented stone workers from Rajasthan and Maharashtra engineered an architectural masterpiece. For nearly four miles, hundreds of sandstone steps run from the top of a 65-foot-high (20-m) escarpment to the base of a temperamental river that swells every year from monsoon rains to swallow the great ghats.

I RETURNED TO DASHASHWAMEDH Ghat before sunrise the next morning. The streets were already filled with women wrapped in magnificent colors, assorted shopkeepers, children selling trinkets, and beggars of every description. The sacred river lay peaceful as the first light of the rising sun revealed the domes, minarets, temples, and nearly ninety ghats that identify the famous Varanasi skyline. The mood and atmosphere along the river was very different than it was just a few short hours before. The intensity of the evening Aarti, the chanting

crowds, and the haunting glow of distant cremation pyres was replaced by the subtle beauty of picturesque masonry, soaring stairways, and the faded pastel paint on the walls of temples and riverfront palaces stretching as far as the eye could see.

Hundreds of people began to emerge from the labyrinth of alleyways making their way down the steep stone steps to begin their day at the river's edge. I again boarded a boat powered by a young oarsman for what would prove to be an unforgettable dawn tour. Men and women of all ages performed their morning rituals while others waded into the river, carefully caressing the water with an unexpected tenderness. As the crowd grew larger the lower steps began to fill with the glorious colors of India. One by one, women entered the river fully clothed for a ritual "dip," displaying an elegant modesty, unaffected by the floating onlookers equipped with digital cameras and video recorders.

The intricate complexity of Varanasi's sacred landscape flows and changes with the currents of time. Every god and every ghat has transcendent importance. There are different ghats for different gods, different religious sects, different castes, and pilgrims from different regions of India. The sacred zone of Varanasi is bound by the Varana River that flows into the Ganges in the north and the Asi River in the south where the 1,550-mile (2,510-km) mother river of India makes a sweeping curve and flows northwards back toward its icy origin in the Himalayas before continuing to its terminus in the Bay of Bengal.

The Hindu name for the Ganges is "Ganga," which is used for both the river and the goddess mistress of Shiva. The Ganges and its tributaries drain a 390,000 square mile (1 million sq km) basin that supports 300 million people in an area with one of the world's highest population densities. But the Ganges is much more than a river; it is symbolic of an Indian culture intertwined with spirituality, history, and tradition unaltered by the constant advance of modernity. What is to many visitors an unbelievably dirty and irreversibly polluted waterway is considered by Hindus to have "ritual purity" and the power to erase many lifetimes of sin.

After floating past dozens of bathing ghats where priests known as "pandas" sit under mushroom-shaped bamboo umbrellas administering to the needs of pilgrims, I again returned to the northern part of the sacred zone and the Manikarnika Ghat. Gone were the beautiful saris and the pious crowds beginning a new day with the rituals of life. The "burning ghat" is a solemn, colorless place under the exclusive dominion of the Doms. For hundreds of years, Dom Raja and his family have been collecting fees for funeral wood, shroud cloths, and even for access to the eternal flame, without which no pyre may be lit. As my boat approached, I could see the shrouded form of a body lying on a bed of logs as a man (presumably the eldest son) dressed in a simple white garment circled the

deceased with twigs of holy kusha grass, lighting the pyre in an ancient cremation rite. Once again I was challenged to suspend judgment and simply experience the spectacle of life and death displayed so publicly along the banks of the Ganges.

As I began to look past the filth and see beyond the broken and disfigured beggars, I began to sense the powerful lure that has drawn pilgrims, poets, writers, philosophers, and intrepid travelers to Varanasi throughout the ages. Along the left bank of the Ganges, between the Varana and Asi rivers, the entirety of human spirituality has played out for nearly three thousand years. It is a place where the past and present have always collided, and the boundaries between life and death are blurred for the devout in search of liberation. It is the birthplace of new ideas, new beliefs, and a repository of ancient rituals. Varanasi has absorbed numerous outside influences, survived countless definitions of "modern," and has also been the victim of destructive forces in a world with different gods and contradictory truths.

Throughout history, from the earliest Aryan nomads from the Ural Mountains and Caucasus who laid a foundation for the Indian social system in 1500 BCE, through often confrontational influences of Arabs, Persians, Mongols, and the British Empire, customs and traditions have been molded and shaped, created and destroyed, but have always emerged as something uniquely Indian. Varanasi is still gripped by centuries-old intolerances and like all of India, struggles to reconcile Gandhian principles of simplicity and austerity with a growing middle class that has an appetite for wealth and the desire to exploit new economic opportunities in the world's largest democracy. Invariably, Varanasi will remain an enigma to Westerners and a paradox for Hindus, but for those who believe, it is where suffering ends through the soft whisper of a living god.

The Sacred City of Shiva

THE LURE Of TIBET

For years I longed to visit Tibet. Maybe it was a fascination inspired by romantic movies or the powerful lure of a distant land of myth and legend that few western travelers have ever seen, but I could barely contain my joy as I crowded at a portal window to steal a momentary glimpse of a magical snow-capped mountain as we made our descent into Gongkar Airport.

I was traveling alone on a spontaneous trip to photograph this beautiful land, but my journey to Tibet began over twenty years ago. I vividly remember being captivated by a fleeting image of the Potala Palace in a television report that described how this isolated and obscure place on the roof of the world was increasingly accessible to a tightly controlled and limited number of outsiders. My pilgrimage started that day.

Just hours after arriving in Lhasa, I felt compelled to disregard the advice of my Chinese tour guide and took a taxi across town to the Potala Palace. I had come from sea level in Beijing to over 12,000 feet (3,657 m) in a matter of hours and was advised to take my first day slowly. But I felt wonderful and wanted to experience a bit of Tibet before I settled into my comfortable room for the night and the controlled itinerary of my guided tour.

The drive down Beijing Road revealed what a large and increasingly modern city Lhasa had become. I was a bit surprised—and a bit disappointed—that the once-forbidden city was now a sprawling mini-metropolis of two hundred thousand people, with contemporary buildings, shopping malls, and nightclubs. I couldn't help but think that perhaps I was too late to experience the Tibet of my romantic vision. That feeling quickly changed to a childlike exhilaration when the Potala came into view through the dusty windows of my Lhasa taxi.

It was late afternoon when I arrived at the Potala, but there were still dozens of pilgrims wandering the streets and prostrating themselves on the sidewalk in front of the towering palace perched high on the terraced slope of the 426-foot (130-m) "Red Hill." I took several photographs of beautiful women who appeared not to be bothered by my camera or my presence as they practiced their faith. The sounds of chanting and the clanking of hand-held prayer wheels would soon become familiar background music, but for now they were an unfamiliar and authentically Tibetan experience that would permeate my dreams for several nights. After a few minutes to absorb the realization that I was actually standing in front of the Potala, I had no trouble waving down a taxi and heading back to the Tibet Hotel.

Following a restless night, I joined my tour group on a series of short excursions to monasteries and sites on the outskirts of Lhasa. On consecutive days, we visited the formerly great Gelugpa (Yellow Hat) monasteries of Sera and Drepung. From the seventeenth century until recently, Drepung was the largest monastic university in the world and home to as many as ten thousand monks.

My visit to Drepung reflected a much different time in the history of this once-magnificent monastery tucked at the base of a hillside just 5 miles (8 km) west of Lhasa. Drepung sustained very little damage during

the Cultural Revolution, and its complex cluster of white buildings with narrow cobblestone roads resembles a small Mediterranean city. I was surprised at how few people we actually encountered. There were very few pilgrims, no other tourists, and although we were told there were seven hundred monks currently in residence, the only monks we met were found sitting in dimly lit corners of the various chapels, diligently thumbing through scriptures while collecting the small twenty yuan fee we were each charged to take pictures.

I shuffled quietly into a small room illuminated by the golden glow of yak-butter candles, when my eyes unexpectedly made contact with an elderly monk. He smiled at me and asked, in perfect English, "Where have you come from?"

"The United States," I answered.

He took my hand as we walked clockwise past a Buddhist shrine and whispered in a voice so quiet I could barely hear, "You have journeyed a very long way to visit Tibet." I was overwhelmed by the warm touch of this graceful man. Before releasing my hand, he looked at me with his gentle smile and instructed, "When you return home, remember to pray for Tibet." It was just my second full day in Lhasa, but at that moment I knew my experience would be unforgettable.

ACCORDING TO LEGEND, Buddhism was received into Tibet's shamanistic warring culture when four hundred Buddhist scriptures fell from the sky onto the roof of the Yumbulagang fortress in the fifth century. Most modern scholars, however, believe that Buddhism was established in Tibet during the reign of King Songtsen Gampo, who died in 650 CE. Under the rule of Songtsen Gampo, Tibetan influence continued to expand through force of arms into inner Asia, northern India, and Nepal. It was also during the time of Songtsen Gampo that Jokhang temple was built in Lhasa.

Although very little remains of the original seventh-century structure, the Jokhang is the holiest of all holy places in Tibet and its layout is ancient. As I listened intently to our guide describe the confusing and unfamiliar icons in the numerous small chapels, I would occasionally feel a little nudge in the small of my back, only to turn and see a tiny Tibetan woman eagerly attempting to pass. In chapel after chapel, devout pilgrims gently made their way past scores of tourists to pay tribute at the altars of

gurus, buddhas, and kings. After spending some time admiring the jeweled statue of Songtsen Gampo, who was flanked by his two wives, I quickly moved through the other chapels of the inner sanctum and followed our guide to the roof before making my way back down to the ground floor and out to the Barkhor.

As I began to explore the Barkhor, Tibet's famous pilgrimage circuit (*kora*), I stopped at the main entrance of the Jokhang. Dusk began to settle over Lhasa. I sat reposed for over an hour on the stone steps that lead down to a forecourt and watched as worshipers, who had traveled for weeks and months to Tibet's most sacred temple, raised their hands in a simple gesture, gently touching their forehead, mouth, and chest before lying prostrate, face down on the stony ground, their hands protected by gloves of wood. The air was fragrant with the smell of incense and human sweat, providing an additional olfactory authenticity to my experience.

I found it hard to leave the forecourt, but the day was nearing an end, so I reluctantly began my swift walk on the Barkhor. In fact, I was literally swept along the circumambulation route by the force of both pilgrims and tourists. The narrow streets were lined with stalls and shops selling butter oil, wicks, *khata* (a silk offering scarf signifying purity and goodwill), and incense for worshipers, as well as cheap jewelry, prayer flags, and assorted other trinkets that I scarcely stopped to notice. Unlike the rhythmic chanting of "*om mani padme hum*" that lifted skyward on the soft breeze in front of the Jokhang, the Barkhor was alive with the sounds of chatter and commerce.

AFTER SEVERAL DAYS EXPLORING monasteries, temples, and shopping areas, we packed our belongings and boarded a comfortable motorcoach for a multiday excursion into the Yarlung Tsangpo Valley. The Yarlung Tsangpo

(Brahmaputra River) is referred to as the "mother river of Tibet." Originating at over 16,000 feet (5,000 m), high in the glaciers of the Himalaya, the Yarlung Tsangpo drains an area of 92,000 square miles (240,000 sq km) with an average elevation of around 14,750 feet (4,500 m), making it the highest river in the world.

Just a short distance outside of Lhasa, we made our first stop, at the Gongkar Chöde Monastery. As we entered the dark inner sanctum of the main assembly hall, we were greeted by the familiar smell of yak-butter candles and the melodic sound of monks at prayer. Several generations of monks sat cross-legged on padded benches, draped in their burgundy and saffron robes, appearing only mildly distracted by the flashes of a dozen camera-clicking onlookers. The sight of tourists moving freely, taking pictures among rows of meditating monks, seemed a bit insensitive, but the opportunity to experience and photograph this solemn scene was irresistible. After nearly a dozen tours of temples and monasteries, I was thrilled to see and hear a room full of monks in an authentic demonstration of piety and devotion.

We spent the night in Zetang Township at a nice hotel in the center of a very poor village on our way to Bayi. From here it was just a short 7.5-mile (12-km) drive the following morning to our next stop at the spectacular Yumbulagang Palace. Yumbulagang rises from the summit of Mt. Tashitseri on the eastern bank of the Yarlung Tsangpo like a medieval European castle. We made several stops along the highway to photograph the towering structure that dominates the Yarlung skyline before our bus stopped at the base of a steep mountain approach.

From the parking area, we were offered an option to walk up the steep switchbacks or ride to the palace on a mule for the affordable fee of ten yuan. There was a small line and a bit of commotion as another group of tourists started up, but without hesitation I mounted my mule and trotted up the mountainside led by a young Tibetan. He held the mule by a short rein and enjoyed having my faithful ride break into a canter on the sharpest hairpin turns. It was a dusty, hot beginning, but once on the top of the hill, it didn't take long to explore the two interior chapels of Yumbulagang.

Inevitably, we began the long journey back to Lhasa through the Mi-La mountain pass, and I started to accept that my Tibetan experience would soon end. The distant sounds of monks chanting, the pervasive odor of yak-butter candles, and the warmth I felt in my soul from the kind toothless smile of a pilgrim, would soon become personal memories from the high plateau that would survive only in my dreams.

I sat quietly as the threatening clouds finally released their rain and one spectacular landscape after another sped past my window like a misty motion picture. Before darkness finally consumed the countryside, we passed several groups of nomads starting yak-dung fires and herding their animals back into camp, following a routine that has been repeated every night for centuries.

We arrived in Lhasa late, but I awoke early the next morning ready to tour the Potala Palace on my last day in Tibet. I was glad that my visit would end at the place that inspired my journey so long ago. But as expected, the three-hundred-fifty-year-old former seat of the Tibetan government and winter palace of the Dalai Lamas is an eerily quiet museum with gift shops offering books and trinkets celebrating the long history of this magnificent building. Scores of tourists and pilgrims lined the dimly lit hallways leading to small rooms and chapels that were once alive with activity.

It felt both awkward and disrespectful to be standing in the doorway, voyeuristically peeking into the private bedroom of the fourteenth Dalai Lama, propped and presented as if he would be returning at any moment. For the first time in my visit, I no longer viewed my experience as a detached traveler drawn by a mystical lure to an enchanting destination. I began to wonder what might have become of Tibet if history had taken a different, less violent, path.

I came to Tibet to see for myself if the magical place of my imagination—filled with ancient rituals, cloistered communities, and an indigenous culture that celebrated a profound spirituality—still existed on the roof of the world. The reality of modern Tibet is obviously very different than my romanticized vision. However, with the promise of increasing autonomy, prayer wheels are again spinning and prayer flags once again release *"om mani padme hum"* to the heavens while monks equipped with cell phones lead the great monastic institutions toward a new partnership with modernity.

OPPOSITE PAGE: Parthenon, Athens, Greece

Chapter 5
Landmarks and Famous Places

*"Though we travel the world over to find the beautiful,
we must carry it with us or we find it not."*

—Ralph Waldo Emerson

The biggest challenge in photographing the world's most visited places is that they are, well, famous. Tourists flock to them from around the world, and every conceivable angle and creative view has been shot and published by a myriad of professional travel photographers. But no two people see the world in the same way. I have stood shoulder-to-shoulder in a group of photographers who all turned out very different images of the same environment.

There is also nothing wrong with making your own version of an iconic photograph from the famous viewpoint. There is a reason that a beautiful view or historic monument makes it onto a postcard or into a guidebook, but it should be only the place to start, not end your photo quest. While historical landmarks and famous places are often links to the past, tourist attractions are also living places. We are free to interact with them in our own way. Our pictures become the reflection of our experience, our visit, a single moment in time when we have a chance to see and photograph something special.

BELOW LEFT TO RIGHT: Wat Yai Chai Mongkhon, Ayutthaya, Thailand; The Hall of Prayer for Good Harvests, Beijing, China; Library of Celsus, Ephesus, Turkey
OPPOSITE PAGE: Juneau, Alaska

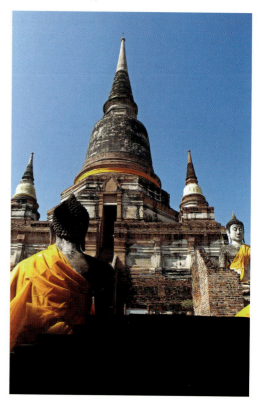  

The Tourist Challenge

As tourists, we often have a predetermined amount of time at any particular attraction, so get the clichéd photograph out of the way and off your mind as soon as possible. You won't feel right until you have found and captured the view just the way you have pictured it in your mind. Then go to work with the time you have left to tell a different story.

Unlike professional travel photographers, tourists don't have the time or ability to scout a unique view across a river or shoot from a nearby rooftop for an unusual perspective. Tourists are restricted to the challenge of the itinerary and confined by their transportation limitations. This is no more evident than in trying to tell the story of a city in one day or of a large sprawling attraction in a matter of hours. If you are adventurous and your escort is willing, you might be able to skip a breakfast or dinner and visit an attraction on your own at sunrise or sunset.

At sites like Chichen Itza, Machu Picchu, the temples of Chiang Mai, or the Forbidden City, I often receive permission to break away from our walking tour and literally run around the site in search of interesting images. I figure I can always research the site further when I get back home. Have I missed some interesting facts, tidbits, or insights my guides might have shared? Probably, but I have only one chance to get the shots. Tours designed specifically for photogra-

phers often account for this from the outset and simply prescribe a time and a rally point, letting everyone explore the site on their own.

So, after taking the typical shots of over-photographed places, find a different point of view or an interesting composition. When the crowd goes right…go left. You might surprise yourself with a totally unique viewpoint. But be sure to circle back to the spot of the iconic shot just before you leave. The light might have changed and can provide you with one last chance at a brilliant photographic souvenir.

Port of Call

There is simply no better way to affordably travel to multiple locations in a short amount of time than on a cruise ship. Wherever there is water, there are cruise opportunities. In just a little over a week you can tour the great cities of Europe on a river cruise, explore vestiges of ancient empires throughout the Mediterranean, or bask in the sunshine on a remote tropical island.

The appeal of a cruise vacation for many tourists is understandable. No travel worries, no need to pack and unpack every day, no need for an alarm clock, and an endless buffet. Unlike a land tour that has a fixed itinerary, when cruisers arrive at a destination, there are a lot of options. Ships have many planned shore excursions that are prepaid, safe, and will guarantee

BELOW: Beijing, China
OPPOSITE PAGE LEFT TO RIGHT: Ayutthaya, Thailand; Beijing, China

you will be back onboard before the ship sails. From adventures like hiking, biking, and kayaking, to sightseeing and cultural tours, shore excursions will provide a glimpse of the location. You will, however, be doing it with a lot of other people.

If you have a specific photographic interest at your next destination or simply don't like the options, an alternative to the packaged shore excursion is to go it alone. Rent a car, scooter, or bike and set out with your camera to explore. Less adventurous photographers can also do a little research and hire a local guide to bring them directly to the points of interest or best spots for photography.

There are a lot of positives about using a cruise ship as transportation for your tourist holiday, but, for a photographer, cruising adds additional complications to the tourist challenge. The biggest is timing. Most ships arrive at a port in the morning, often not disembarking until hours after sunrise. Equally frustrating to photographers trying to utilize the light of the golden hour, most ships have already disembarked and are well out to sea by the time the sun begins to set. This makes for a beautiful and romantic moment onboard, but leaves photographers a featureless ocean sunset to shoot.

A good way to approach cruise tour photography is as an editorial photographer. Tell the complete story of your experience. Photograph the landscapes of the ship and other passengers as they enjoy onboard features. Many ship tours can bring you behind the scenes of the galley or entertainment. Find interesting ways to use the ship as a background for portraits and action shots. All around the ship lie potential narrative photographs to create as you journey to your next port of call.

More to the Story

There are some landmarks that are so recognizable that a single image can define a place. It is impossible to visit Paris and not shoot the Eiffel tower. Who wouldn't recognize the Taj Mahal or the Great Wall of China? But don't try to tell the entire story of a wonderful travel experience in a single picture. The story of a historic place is often complex, with both a past and present. It will take a series of images to illustrate both the historic significance that made it famous and its modern complexity.

When I enter a site, I almost always start by finding the iconic shots and then work back to add depth to my destination story as time permits. The pictures published in guidebooks,

Controlling Focus

Unlike a camera, the human eye can't focus on both close and distant objects at the same time. A reason that novice photographers don't often notice the strange pole coming out of the subjects' ear before making a portrait is because they quite literally didn't see it in the background. If we focus our eyes on something close to us (like your hand out in front of you), everything behind it is blurry. If we shift our focus to the background, the foreground object is blurry. We naturally understand this visual limitation, which allows a photographer to introduce depth through a foreground blur.

When everything in the picture is equally sharp, the viewer relies on elements of design and composition to navigate the image. If some parts of the image are sharp and others not, the eye is drawn to the sharpest parts of the image. Controlling focus is one of the most important skills for any photographer. If you leave the choice of f-stop to the automatic settings of your camera, you will have surrendered control of one of the most significant aspects of photography. As photographers, we control our depth of field to reduce visual clutter and let viewers know what is important in the image.

Depth of Field

The discussion of depth of field is often intimidating for novice photographers. Generally, the larger the lens aperture (smaller f-number), the more shallow the depth of field, and the smaller the aperture (larger f-number), the greater the depth of field. Longer focal-length lenses also compress space and have a shallower depth of field than wide-angle lenses. When shooting a landscape or street scene, you will typically want as much of the image in focus as possible. Taking a portrait or attempting to manipulate the viewpoint using selective focus will put emphasis on areas of the image that you choose.

When you look through the lens, however, you are not seeing what will be sharp in the photograph. Understand that you are looking through the lens at its largest aperture (f/2.8, f/4, etc.). If your camera is set to f/11 or f/16, the resulting photograph will be very different from what you see. Many DSLR's have a depth-of-field preview button, but the only way to see what is sharp and what is not with a rangefinder point-and-shoot is to take a picture and look at it. My way of controlling depth of field is to use the aperture preferred settings of my cameras.

Chapter Five

OPPOSITE PAGE LEFT TO RIGHT: Colosseum, Rome, Italy; Santorini, Greece
RIGHT: Santa Ana Cathedral, Valladolid, Mexico

magazine articles, and tourist postcards are often harder to find than you might think. I remember climbing up and down stairs in the winding small alleyways of the Greek island of Santorini thinking, "Where the heck did they get that shot?" I could see the picturesque church I was stalking, but I just couldn't find the perfect spot. It was very frustrating!

Once you do find the perfect spot, don't settle for an entirely literal interpretation. Changing your viewpoint even a little can result in a very different photograph. Finding a new way to show a landmark can be as simple as framing through the branches of a tree, shooting into the sun, or including surrounding architecture. Look for a reflection in a window, shoot it as a silhouette, or crop it tight to show details.

Besides the obvious, I look for colors, textures, signs, people, and clothing. I look for subjects that tell a story about the place and culture I am visiting. Train yourself to look for those unconventional frames. A young couple walking holding hands, a worker sweeping the floor, a beautiful child waiting in line in the arms of her father, or a monk tending to a garden all help complete the story. A human element will give the scene context that will captivate viewers more deeply than the simple shot of a landmark.

This Place is Ruined

It takes real imagination to gaze upon a pile of old rocks and envision an ancient culture in all of its glory. The history and intrigue of ancient ruins are a huge draw for tourists and can be a rich and interesting photographic subject. Walls, arches, and columns are the elements of a human story. Once upon a time people strolled the cobblestone roads of Pompeii, gladiators did battle on the floor of the Colosseum, athletes from around the world competed at Olympia, and emperors ruled over what are now lost civilizations.

It also takes imagination to approach a pile of rubble and create photographs that will build a story of the past by the fragments left behind.

The ruins of antiquity we visit as tourists are often the remnants of buildings that were the containers of life. Sites like those of the Maya and Inca in Central and South America were long ago abandoned with little or no hint as to the complex relationship to their surroundings. Roman ruins span the entire length of the once great empire. They feed our curiosity as we walk through places that were once teeming with life.

Luckily, many amazing ruins have been partially reconstructed, or there are abundant areas where nature hasn't completely taken over. Placing them in context can, however, be tricky. It is tempting to pull back to relate the subject to the landscape, but don't go so far that you end up taking a picture of nothing at all. Details

The Blind Shot

One way to play with new angles is to raise the camera over your head, place it on the ground and point it up, or shoot from your hip as you walk. The advent of auto focus has allowed photographers to get a sharp image without having to look through the viewfinder. Creating blind shots like these does require a good understanding of framing and being able to envision what the camera might be pointing at. A little luck also helps.

There are times when lying down on the ground to shoot up isn't practical or might be culturally insensitive. To get a shot looking up an expanse, put the camera on the ground, point it, and shoot blind. I have also used the blind shot while walking or hiking to see the world from a different angle. I walk along with the camera as low as possible and fire off a few shots as we move.

We have all seen news photographers in a scrum of other photographers holding their camera up over the head firing off shots at an unfolding event. It is also a great technique for a travel photographer navigating through the large crowds at an attraction. The over-the-head shot can give a great perspective and the often-tilted horizon can add additional tension to a crowded location.

The blind shot can also give your photographs a voyeuristic feel or visual tension when made by holding the camera at your side or waist while walking a down a crowded street or through a market. Shooting blind by placing it on a table or in your lap at a restaurant can also provide interesting results. The resulting compositions are often more edgy and creative than if you would have selected the framing by looking through the viewfinder.

OPPOSITE PAGE: Beijing, China
BELOW LEFT TO RIGHT: Louvre Museum, Paris, France; Taj Mahal, Agra, India

Landmarks and Famous Places 115

OPPOSITE PAGE: Chichen Itza, Mexico
BELOW: Pompeii, Italy

often communicate more than the whole. Small touches in tile or stonework, or a faded painting on a wall or ceiling can remind us that humans once lived here. Roots growing through and over walls can provide a dramatic sense of the passing of time and contrasting texture.

Most ancient ruins we visit were built in the days before electric lights and are often beautifully lit with natural light. They were designed and constructed to utilize the daily rise and fall of the sun. Light coming through windows and across archways can illuminate interior spaces as the occupants experienced them. It is always nice to have a beautiful blue sky and the warmth of sunlight when photographing a historic place, but an overcast or rainy day might add a sense of mystery. Remember that if you are experiencing less than perfect weather, the original inhabitants lived under similar conditions.

Photographing the Tourists' Experience

Since famous attractions are often crowded with people, it can be virtually impossible to find a composition that isn't jam-packed with other tourists. You can be patient and wait for a moment when your viewfinder is uncluttered by the tourist mass or use the other tourists to provide a focal point and add interest to your overall composition.

Using silhouettes and placing people in the foreground of your shots can give perspective and scale to statues and buildings. Framing people in the image also suggests that you are not alone, adding movement to a living place. Some of my favorite shots are photographs of other tourists interacting with the site in their own way, often photographing other tourists photographing other tourists. These are opportunities to make images where time and culture overlap.

There are also many chances to create interesting narrative photographs as you literally travel through your itinerary. Modes of travel are an important part of the tourist experience. Shots from the top of a tour bus, or from a rickshaw or *tuk tuk* can also add a bit of fun and tension by framing the image from the point of view of a participant. Try shooting over the shoulder of another tourist.

Landmarks and Famous Places

FIELD NOTES

Awakening the Dragon

At the north end of Beihai Park in Beijing, the massive Nine Dragon Wall stands as a testament to a time when superstition determined the course of daily life in the heart of one of the world's oldest civilizations. The center of the 250-year-old wall is dominated by a large dragon flanked and intertwined with eight other giant beasts in a tile mosaic representing the nine legendary sons of the Chinese dragon.

The Chinese dragon is the bringer of rain, wealth, and good luck. It has long been a potent symbol of imperial power, wisdom, and strength. In ancient times, the sighting of a dragon was a sign from heaven confirming the achievements of a benevolent ruler. Emperors embraced the myth and paid handsomely for accounts of dragon sightings in their dominion. It is the dragon that watches over and protects the people of China and her walls.

Winding like a giant dragon across mountains, forests, and deserts for almost 5,500 miles (8,850 km) of northern China is the enduring Chinese icon of myth and legend: The Great Wall of China. While sections of "wild wall" are now in ruins, the Great Wall is one of the man-made wonders of the world.

Construction of the wall began over two thousand years ago by the rulers of independent kingdoms who linked their earthen barricades together in a largely unsuccessful attempt to keep out marauding nomadic warriors. The wall is not a continuous structure, but a patchwork of separate sections built in a nearly continuous eighteen hundred-year construction project. Many of the more accessible and recently rebuilt sections of the wall near Beijing were constructed during the Ming dynasty (1368–1644), whose rulers lived and governed from the growing city following the era of Genghis Khan.

Khan, the infamous Mongolian warrior, invaded Beijing in 1215 CE and reduced the small isolated city to rubble. By 1279, Kublai Khan, the grandson of Genghis, reigned over the largest empire the world has ever known from his imperial palace on the spot where the Forbidden City currently sits.

Constructed in accordance with Confucian principles of yin and yang by the third emperor of the Ming dynasty, the Forbidden City was off limits to the masses, concealed behind a 170-foot-wide (52-m) moat and 32-foot-high (10-m) wall. Today, Chinese families join tourists from around the world joyfully snapping souvenir photographs in front of the sweeping cluster of intricately adorned buildings in the formally cloistered imperial palace where twenty-four emperors ruled China for nearly five hundred years.

In a city protected by walls within walls, remain some of the oldest neighborhoods in Beijing, called *hutongs*. Many of the narrow residential alleyways have been demolished in the name of modernization, but in isolated pockets around the city, the sounds and smells of old Beijing are alive with authenticity. Flanked by modern skyscrapers and futuristic architecture, Beijing's hutongs are a disappearing cultural treasure and a remnant of the city's fourteenth-century design. These charming alleyways provide travelers a fleeting glimpse at a simple and ancient way of life.

Within and around Beijing lie many of China's most stunning attractions: the Forbidden City, the Lama Temple, the Summer Palace and, of course, the Great Wall. But the historic icons of Beijing tell only a small part of what is a long and human story. Displayed quietly amidst daily life in hutongs and night markets, or on full display in a performance of Beijing Opera, the enduring culture of China is visible in the portraits of her people.

As the curious descend upon China, China is also looking outward as never before, engaging the global community and inviting the world to visit. Ever so slowly, the physical and intellectual walls of isolation are turning into windows of opportunity and understanding as one-and-a-half billion people struggle to define their new identity while retaining their ancient culture in the shadow of a modern dragon designed with glass and steel.

FIELD NOTES

The Lost City of the Inca

We walked for days over and around some of South America's most stunning and inaccessible mountains. We walked as the Inca did, step by step toward a mysterious destination that has captivated the world since 1911. After one final ascent of a massive wall of stacked and broken granite, we passed through Intipunku, the Sun Gate, and stood motionless, staring down at the cloud-shrouded enigma of the Inca. We breathlessly marveled at the small collection of stones nestled in the saddle between two peaks of a narrow ridge. We had arrived at Machu Picchu.

Our journey to the fabled lost city started on a beautiful spring day in the Andés. My wife and I set out from camp near the train depot at Kilometer 88 to trek the Inca Trail with seven other tourist-trekkers, our lead guide Narcico, fifteen Peruvian porters, and a fabulous cook. The trail is a collection of ancient Inca footpaths, which have traversed the mountain landscape of the Andes for over four hundred years, interwoven with recently cut connector trails that meander through densely forested foothills in the shadows of snow-covered peaks.

It is believed by many that Machu Picchu was a royal retreat for Inca nobility in Cuzco, built during the reign of Pachacútec, a place of spiritual and ceremonial significance, or possibly the administrative center for a well-populated region. It would have been no more than a small town by Inca standards; home to less than one thousand people at its peak. It is still a mystery as to why the Spanish never found the hidden jewel of the Andés. Some believe that it was abandoned and its memory lost even to the Amerindians of the region before the conquistadors arrived. The entire mountain masterpiece was built, settled, and abandoned in less than one hundred years. We may never know why.

When Yale professor of history Hiram Bingham stumbled upon the jungle-covered ruins at Machu Picchu in July 1911, he was actually searching for the legendary lost city of Vilcabamba. Vilcabamba was a remote mountain refuge created for fleeing Inca nobility as the conquistadors made their way south into Cuzco. Bingham was looking for the last stronghold of a conquered people. What he found was something very different.

Following a narrow mule trail through the Urubamba Gorge, Bingham was led by a local farmer to a site 2,000 feet (670 m) above the river at a place the locals called "ancient peak." Bingham later wrote: "In the dense shadow, hiding in bamboo thickets and tangled vines, could be seen, here and there, walls of white granite ashlars most carefully cut and exquisitely fitted together…would anyone believe what I had found?"

It was late afternoon when I finally had my chance to see Bingham's lost city for myself. We had just over an hour to roam amidst the ruins, still burdened by our packs and trail-worn clothing. Day trippers who came up on one of the rail services from Cuzco had already started their return, providing us the chance to contemplate the mysterious wonder of this place nearly alone as the day neared its end. As I sat on the terraced slopes watching the remaining tourists head for the buses that would take them down to the tourist hub of Aguas Calientes, I could picture thousands of Inca scurrying about doing daily chores and worshiping their gods in the most picturesque small town on earth.

A century has passed since Hiram Bingham introduced the world to Machu Picchu. Today, thousands of tourists are transported to the once forgotten city on a luxury train that bears his name. A new city has emerged to support a growing tourism industry along the banks of the Urubamba River near where he camped, and resilient descendants of the Inca continue to live simply in the Peruvian highlands, only marginally connected to the national economy.

Romantic Expectations

After checking into Hotel Palazzo Giovanelli, we dropped our bags and headed on foot toward the Rialto Bridge. We navigated the maze of narrow alleyways guided by signs posted at street corners pointing the way to important landmarks. The labyrinth of shady passages soon released us into the crowded enthusiasm of modern Venice. Cries of uniformed boatmen rose above the din of tourist commotion as we consumed our first excited look at the iconic 160-foot span (50-m). Thousands of people, boats, gondolas, cafés, and restaurants lined the bustling canal. Couples of all ages posed for digital snapshots as proof of their presence in Europe's most romantic city.

I'm not a romantic guy. I know that about myself. So when my wife suggested we spend our twentieth wedding anniversary in Venice, I feared that her expectations might be way too high. But after years of following me to remote locations where dung is still being used as a building material, this year I simply had no choice but to follow Barbara's romantic muse. We climbed to the center of the bridge to take our turn admiring the famous view amid the crush of tourists. Below us, barges delivered supplies, water taxis ferried passengers, and gondoliers entertained as they have since the eleventh century. We enjoyed only a glimpse down the

Grand Canal before being gently repositioned by the next wave of enthusiastic gawkers. Overwhelmed by the theme-park atmosphere, we quickly decided to escape the crowd and take a quiet stroll through the nearly empty neighborhoods just a stone's throw away.

The area around the Rialto Bridge takes its name from *rivo alto* (high bank) and was one of the first parts of Venice to be settled. The city was founded in 421 CE following the dedication of the San Giacomo Church on what was then the islet of Rialto. At first, Venice was a group of united lagoon communities fleeing invaders from the north during the last years of the Western Roman Empire. Over the centuries it grew into an improbable place, built on more than one hundred small islands interconnected by four hundred bridges. Millions of closely spaced foundation timbers driven through soft layers of sand and mud support the many baroque and renaissance buildings.

The city is divided into six administrative districts or *sestieri*. The district directly west of the Rialto Bridge, where Barbara and I went wandering, is known as San Polo. It was historically the commercial quarter, once lined with stalls selling exotic spices, fabrics from the East, and bounty from the sea. Today, it is primarily a residential area dotted with churches and piazzas (public squares). It wasn't long before our jet lag caught up with us and we were hopelessly lost, tired, and hungry. In the distance we noticed a row of square tables draped with white cloth next to the glow of an open doorway. "Food" we announced simultaneously.

It was still a bit early for dinner, so we weren't sure if the restaurant was even open. A handwritten sign posted at Trattoria Antiche Carampane read: "No Lasagne, No Pizza. No Menú Turistico."

"Perfect," we agreed. A smiling, slightly balding middle-aged man appeared in the doorway as we attempted to sneak

a peek inside. "Ciao…please…come in," he said in heavily accented English. He proceeded to ask us where we were from and led us to a small table in a back room. No doubt we looked like lost and confused tourists. During a slight pause in his review of the night's menu, I glanced over at Barbara and said, "We will have whatever you recommend." "Va bene," he replied with a wink of approval and turned toward the kitchen.

Soon a bottle of wine and a small paper cone arrived overflowing with tiny fried shrimp. Within a half hour, several groups were seated and the small dining room was almost completely filled. I was nearly shoulder-to-shoulder with an older Italian gentleman named Piero, who commented that this was his favorite restaurant in all of Venice. The tables were so close together, it was almost impossible not to greet and share the experience with neighbors.

We lingered for over an hour laughing and sharing stories with a small group before making our way back to our hotel. By the time we left the trattoria, the sun had dipped below the horizon, leaving only the soft hue of twilight and eerie pockets of orange/yellow light to illuminate our retreat. The streets were quiet. Day-trippers had long ago returned to their beach resorts or found their way back to their cruise ships. We walked the quaint cobblestone corridors virtually alone.

OUR NIGHT WAS INTENTIONALLY SHORT. We woke with the sun on the morning of our anniversary and left the hotel without even taking a moment to explore the sixteenth-century palace that would be our luxury base camp before boarding our ship for a Mediterranean cruise. We chose the newly renovated four-star hotel because it was far away from the tourist craziness of the Rialto and right next to the San Stae stop of the public waterbus known as the vaporetto. Different lines of boats travel up and down the Grand Canal, making convenient stops at well-marked docks along the way. Visitors can buy a single-ride ticket or passes of different durations that allow unlimited use from one day to one week.

We shuttled back to the Rialto Bridge on the vaporetto just minutes after sunrise. The bridge was completely empty of tourists. For a moment, Barbara and I had a private platform to witness the subtle splendor of Venice. A sprinkling of gondolas dotted the peaceful canal, leaving a small ripple in their wake as they glided across the calm waters. Cafés served steaming cups of cappuccino to early risers. The city's workers began to arrive and shopkeepers prepared for the daily onslaught of visitors.

The banks of the Grand Canal are lined with more than one hundred seventy buildings, most of which were built between the thirteenth and the eighteenth centuries. Many combined a residential palace with a business office and a warehouse at water level. At the peak of its power and wealth in the thirteenth century, Venice was the most prosperous city in all of Europe and controlled a vast sea-empire in the Mediterranean. During this time, the wealthiest families vied to build the most spectacular palace along the Grand Canal. As the first light of day touched the historic old palaces, we were given a hint at this glorious past.

The Venetian Republic survived for over a thousand years until it fell to Napoleon in 1797. After the fall, construction of housing in Venice was suspended. The cinematic scene unfolding below us would have looked very much the same to couples standing on the bridge at sunrise for the past two hundred years. From a distance, the elegant decay of what could easily become an overcrowded tourist trap is eclipsed by the sentimental fantasy to escape into the romantic premodern world of our imagination, even if only for a few short hours.

We slowly made our way back to the vaporetto and rode a short distance to Piazza San Marco (Saint Mark's Square). Dozens of gondolas lined the edge of the canal, cloaked in their protective royal blue coverings. We passed local art students sitting in the golden glow of the rising sun sketching the timeless landscape at the mouth of the Grand Canal. Before entering the famous square, we detoured into the back streets of the San Marco district. Small bridges led us to rows of sleeping houses adorned with colorful flowerboxes below shuttered windows. Peeling plaster and weathered brick added texture and context to the aging façades.

By the time we returned to Piazza San Marco, there was a small but growing line of people waiting for the first tours of the spectacular Palazzo

Ducale (Doge's Palace). Piazza San Marco is the most famous public square in Venice and contains two of the city's most important sights: the Basilica di San Marco and Palazzo Ducale.

We didn't plan to stay long in the square. We had plenty of time to do the tours another day, so this morning we found a small café for a cup of cappuccino and to admire the exterior sights of the piazza. Throughout the long history of the grand square, it has been the social, political, and religious gathering place of the city. The Basilica of Saint Mark's is the most famous church in Venice and is considered one of the best-known examples of Byzantine architecture. Built in the eleventh century, the present church is the third on the site and said to have been decorated with the booty of returning sea captains. For centuries, merchant ships were required by law to bring back a precious gift for the so-called "House of Saint Mark."

WE ESCAPED BACK TO OUR HOTEL just before the massive cruise ships dumped camera-laden newcomers into the piazza. The bulk of the cruise ship passengers arrive in Venice along with tours from mainland hotels at around 10:00 a.m. By then, Barbara and I were safely back at our hotel having a late breakfast and planning the remainder of our day. After our midday siesta, we made the mistake of returning to Piazza San Marco a bit too early.

Roughly twenty-two million tourists come to Venice each year and almost all of them find their way to the piazza. When we arrived via the crowded vaporetto, we were pretty sure all twenty-two million were in the square that day. We returned to the piazza for a very specific purpose. Barbara had spotted a couple jewelry stores off the piazza in the morning and wanted to shop before our early anniversary dinner. We quickly found what she was looking for, a small gold gondola pendant for her bracelet.

Romantic Expectations   **127**

The gondola is an unmistakable symbol of Venice. For centuries, gondolas were the chief means of transportation. To prevent an ostentatious competition of individual wealth, an official decree in 1592 forever called for all gondolas to be painted black. It is estimated that there were eight to ten thousand gondolas on the waters of Venice during the seventeenth and eighteenth centuries. Today, along with being able to maneuver the gondola through the tight spaces of Venetian canals, gondoliers must possess foreign language skills and pass a comprehensive exam on Venetian history and landmarks.

Ever since we arrived, we had considered whether or not we would take the expensive boat ride. We watched as stripe-shirted singing gondoliers maneuvered the traditional flat-bottomed boats in and out of tight canals. We witnessed irritated boatmen negotiate traffic jams to the amusement of tourist-onlookers, and we waved at slightly embarrassed kids as they passed by us on the Grand Canal. It looked like fun, but not the charming and romantic experience of legend.

A ride was probably inevitable, but it wasn't high on my "must-do" list as we once again strolled through the endless maze in the direction of the Rialto Bridge. To our surprise, we suddenly hit a dead end. The ally we had ventured down stopped at a stairwell leading to a gondola station with two boats sitting empty. It was an impossible coincidence. Barbara looked at me and smiled from ear to ear. Serendipity had intervened. I summoned my inner Casanova as a gondolier approached. After settling on a time and a price, we entered the charming back canals for our forty-minute float in Europe's most romantic city.

OPPOSITE PAGE: Mount Cook, New Zealand

Chapter 6
Nature's Spectacle

"Our happiest moments as tourists always seem to come when we stumble upon one thing while in pursuit of something else."

—Lawrence Block

There is nothing quite like driving through the East African plains at sunset or awaking to witness a spectacular sunrise in the Himalaya. Our planet has blessed photographers with a vast range of landscapes. Capturing oceans, deserts, glaciers, geysers, volcanoes, rainforests, and all of the subtle nuances of nature in between is often where we begin our love affair with photography. Photographing nature is also where most of us first learn that recording a location is very different than capturing a moment in time as an artist. Reducing a stunning or ephemeral panorama into a two-dimensional pictorial representation is often a disappointing experience. There is simply no way to photographically express a feeling.

The magical feeling that grips us when surrounded by the high peaks of a mountain landscape or when gazing empathetically into the eyes of an equally curious animal are the special and very personal moments of travel. Photography is a different experience; it tells its own story—a story intended to paint a beautiful or illustrative picture from the scene as it is encountered. Done well, our photographs of nature's wonders can begin to share our personal connection with the natural world and remind us that we are part of a larger, ongoing story that has shaped life on our planet since the beginning of time.

BELOW: Negev Desert, Israel
OPPOSITE PAGE: Namib Desert, Namibia; Hopkins, Belize

Seeing the Light

Controlling light is the essence of photography. The better you are at recognizing the direction and quality of light, the better you will become at mastering light and dark. The quality of light is perhaps the most important aspect of a successful landscape photograph, but tourist photographers don't always have the luxury to wait for the ideal natural light. Stumbling upon light that is dramatic or moody is a matter of chance, but even in less than ideal circumstances, you do have some control. Simply watching the sun and waiting for clouds to come and go is the quickest way to alter both the color and intensity of light.

As clouds pass, the scene changes considerably. Under full sun, highlights and shadows add contrast, texture, and graphic elements. At the edges of clouds, the intensity is reduced but color and direction remain. A cloud is like placing a giant diffuser over the light source, eliminating shadows and cooling the color temperature, which might be perfect for working in a forest or where natural colors are already intense.

Clouds also add pockets of contrast to a landscape scene as areas pop in and out of sunlight. By watching the movement of sun and clouds, emphasis can be repositioned around the image in a matter of moments, resulting in very different photographs. If, however, you are stuck with one lighting situation, like the soft diffusion of an overcast sky or the strong midday sun, the only option is to match your conditions to a compatible subject.

Harsh midday light creates impossible contrast between highlights and shadows. The human eye and brain have the ability to adapt our vision and see detail as we glance in and out of shadows—the camera does not. In a high-contrast scene, photographers need to make a choice to expose for shadows or highlights. No matter how good your camera is, it will not be able to record the entire tonal range of the more challenging lighting situations you encounter.

Recognizing the situation is key. You might need to frame the photograph to emphasize one light condition or change the apparent

Nature's Spectacle   **133**

BELOW: **Dead Sea, Israel**
OPPOSITE PAGE TOP TO BOTTOM: **Negev Desert, Israel; South Island, New Zealand**

direction of light by changing your shooting position. If you choose to showcase a subject in shadow, your highlights will go completely white. Conversely, if you expose for the brightest area of your subject, the shadows will go black, with little or no detail. Both choices can lead to amazing images. Used properly, harsh shadows can also be great design elements for creating lines, shapes, and forms.

Landscapes and Scenics

Mother Nature can be very patient. The landscapes we capture at 1/250th of a second took thousands or millions of years to create. Some are distinctive of a particular place, like a mountain range, desert, canyon, rainforest, waterfall, or seascape. Others take on a temporary beauty or magical quality by the whims of local weather. Landscape photography is ultimately all about the quality of light. A new and completely different version of a landscape can be seen under different weather conditions, at different times of day, and different times of year.

Technically, landscapes can be among the least complicated photographic subjects. Unlike a busy market or crowded attraction, the world moves much slower when a scenic vista is your subject, and Mother Nature rarely refuses a portrait. Morning and evening are often considered the best times of day for scenic photographs, but less than perfect atmospheric conditions can change the quality of the image. Mist and fog create softness and depth as distant objects are obscured. Foreground objects will add dimensionality, and shadows will reveal texture in any landscape. Fast shutter speeds will capture motion, and long exposures will turn turbulent water into a flowing web of silk.

Compositionally, however, landscape photographs can be very challenging. The difficulty is to find a subject or an anchor that will lead the viewer into the image. It can be a tree on the horizon, a line, object, color, shape, or form, but a successful landscape or scenic photograph must be "of something" and tell a story just like any other narrative image. A sense of depth is

Using Lines

Lines are powerful design elements, and when intentionally controlled, they function like arrows leading the eye to certain areas of the image. Lines also express through their character and direction, and trigger unconscious emotional reactions in the viewer. Horizontal lines project stability and tranquility. Compositions dominated by horizontal lines tend to feel quiet and calm. Vertical lines communicate strength and power, and diagonals suggest action and movement. Likewise, soft gentle curves have a sensual quality suggesting grace and relaxation, while sharp or acute curves display confusion or chaos.

    Controlling lines in the composition of a photograph requires that you see them through the viewfinder and place them to their greatest effect. Lines exist all around us. Roads, fences, buildings, shorelines, and canals all are composed of lines. Once you become conscious of lines, you will begin to see them everywhere. If you are trying to create stability in a landscape or cityscape, your horizon should be parallel to the edge of the frame. To create the immediate sensation of tension, shift the horizon off axis or change your angle of view to force an unnatural perspective.

Nature's Spectacle   **135**

Exposure

We control light through exposure. With the sophistication of today's modern cameras, a good exposure is pretty simple under normal conditions—just set the camera to automatic and start shooting. It is trickier when conditions aren't normal. Most cameras have options for exposure control. They take readings from around the image and make recommendations about the exposure. Camera metering systems respond well when a scene is front-lit with the sun at your back, but be careful if your subject is backlit by a bright sky or if the scene is generally bright or dark; your meter will be fooled.

Metering systems will interpret the scene in front of the camera and then set the exposure to make it a midtone gray. So, if the scene is generally bright, the meter will read a lot of light and make it darker—underexposing shadows (this is why you get silhouetted portraits if the background sky is bright). If the scene is generally dark, the meter will read very little light and make it lighter—overexposing bright areas. Most modern digital cameras do allow you to change the area within the frame that the system uses to judge the scene. Matrix metering will interpret the entire scene, accounting for highlights and shadows, while spot meters will focus only on a small, defined area of your choosing.

If your meter is having a problem properly exposing a high-contrast scene, try switching to a spot-meter setting and point your meter at the place in the frame that you want properly exposed to a midtone gray. Many cameras also have an exposure lock, so you can lock in the exposure for the shadows or highlights and then reframe your shot. Check your manuals.

often created by the landscape itself, so keeping all the elements of the image sharp by using a small aperture is usually preferred. A tripod can be valuable to compensate for a slower shutter speed, and the exposure is often set for the midtones of the general scene.

Human elements like a farmhouse, a fence, a lighthouse, or a person walking in the distance can provide depth and scale to a vast expanse. A human element will also overlay a cultural significance by introducing an essential spirit of a place and time. Some of the world's most stunning landscapes are called "home" by many. They are the backgrounds of people's lives.

Golden Hour

One of the true thrills of travel photography is capturing a dramatic light effect when the color, direction, and intensity perfectly coalesce into a spectacular picture. Sometimes, this happens before or after a storm or when the sun and atmosphere interact in brief and sudden phenomena, but the best way to increase your odds of capturing the drama of natural light is to rise before the sun and watch as it dips below the horizon at day's end.

Photographers call it the golden, or magic, hour, the time of day around sunrise and sunset when the sun is low on the horizon and the sky takes on soft colors, beautifying and romanticizing virtually any scene. Early risers are familiar with the soft hues of color just before the sun breaks the horizon, and patient landscape pho-

LEFT: Inle Lake, Myanmar

tographers are rewarded moments before sunset as the long dark shadows and golden glow accentuate each topographical nuance.

The reality of the golden hour is more accurately that there is about one half-hour of perfect shooting time in the morning and one half-hour at dusk. The theatrics of light as the setting sun nears the horizon disappear into darkness remarkably fast. Likewise, it doesn't take long before the soft, flattering light of sunrise takes on the same quality as a midday sun.

Embracing White

Becoming a better photographer isn't always just about learning new techniques or honing your eye. Sometimes, it means putting yourself in the right place at the right time to get the best shot under the best conditions. Tours specifically designed for photographers often have a plan to do just that, but you can't always count on Mother Nature to cooperate. Some days you might just be unlucky. But that doesn't mean you put down your camera and stop shooting.

Unfortunately, some of the world's great things to see and places to visit also have overcast and stormy days. When those days happen during your tour, you need to think about the images you can make, not the ones you had hoped to make. Romantic, muted tones and soft light can provide pleasant modeling to facial features in your portraits. Wet streets and umbrellas can add drama to everyday city scenes. Threatening skies can generate feelings of excitement and anticipation to a seascape. Monochromatic

A Filtered Effect

If you shoot a lot over many years, you begin to develop a style. We all see the world differently, so it is not surprising that the look and feel of our pictures will vary greatly. Since my photography is primarily used to share travel adventures with others in magazine and online narratives, I strive to present a look that is natural and believable. While there is often a gap between what our eye sees and what the camera can record, I rarely use strong filters, I don't blend multiple exposures through high-dynamic-range imaging (HDR), and I avoid unnatural saturation and other computer manipulations that dramatically alter the scene.

My preferred way to deal with a washed out sky or broad tonal range on a bright day is to use a graduated neutral density filter in front of my lens to darken the sky a bit before I bring the shot into my computer. I will also use warm colored graduated filters on occasion to enhance a sunset or add a little extra drama to a silhouette. And I do make use of the computer's ability to tweak my images into a pleasing or more dramatic presentation through Highlight and Shadow, Contrast, and Saturation. While I am not a purest as to image manipulation, I try to use the tools that modern digital photography offers with a gentle touch.

OPPOSITE PAGE TOP TO BOTTOM:
Galápagos Islands, Ecuador; Inle Lake, Myanmar
BELOW: Iceland

When you have overcast and stormy days during your tour, you need to think about the images you can make, not the ones you had hoped to make.

landscapes can have dramatic effects. Dense fog can elicit a feeling of foreboding as objects fade layer after layer into the misty distance.

A bright sun isn't always necessary to create an interesting image. If you know what to look for and how to use it, an overcast day can be a great friend to travel photographers.

The diffusion of an overcast sky, "nature's soft box," is often perfect for architectural details where the subtle changes in color and texture carry the visual interest. Markets and street portraits, as well as many landscapes, nature, and wildlife scenes, also benefit from the soft, balanced light, where sunlight can create severe highlights and shadows.

A white sky can also be used like a studio photographer would use a white background to showcase a product. Line, shape, form, and color will pop off the neutral background and the sky becomes negative space in your composition. Since the sky is already white, you don't need to fear overexposure, but you will need to take care to properly expose for the subject.

Local Wildlife

There is a truth I tell to all of the photographers who join me on a safari. It is that most of the time, very little happens in the wild. And when something incredible does actually happen, it rarely coincides with the exact moment you are there. Professional wildlife photographers spend weeks, if not months, patiently waiting for one amazing moment with a cheetah, lion, or leopard. The great predators of the African savanna can spend up to twenty hours a day… sleeping. They most often ply their craft under the cover of darkness.

Finding elusive animals provides its own challenge, but when you do come across the animals of your interest, you can't ask them to

Nature's Spectacle

OPPOSITE PAGE LEFT TO RIGHT: Samburu, Kenya; Wellington, New Zealand
BELOW: Maasai Mara, Kenya

do something interesting or look cute because the group is about to move on. Wild animals do what they do, when they do it. We can only put ourselves in a position to see it when it happens and enjoy the events of nature we are lucky enough to photograph.

Much like our tourist images of people, photographs of wildlife will fall into three primary categories: a portrait, an environmental portrait, and scenes of everyday life. As with a compelling portrait of a person, life is often revealed through the eyes. Eye contact isn't always possible, but the inquisitive gaze of a young animal or the confrontational stare of a predator will make for an arresting image. Similarly, photographing wildlife in their natural environments shows how the animal lives and interacts with the landscape.

The longer you have at a location with professional guides, the more likely you will see something special or capture something incredibly rare. But there are also wonderful photographs to be created during quiet moments when animals are following their daily routine, foraging for food, instructing their young, or engaging in a courtship ritual, unaffected by our presence. In a very short period of time, you can learn to understand their habits and even recognize the personalities of different individuals.

Some places in the world, like the African Serengeti, Yellowstone National Park in the United States, and the Galápagos Islands of Ecuador, are famous wildlife destinations, but interesting animals can be found in almost every travel destination. They are a part of our lives. They are beasts of burden, cultural icons, and a domesticated part of the local landscape. Horses in Iceland, sheep in New Zealand, camels and cows in India, and llamas in Peru are an important part of the destination narrative. Residents of the tiny Greek Island of Mykonos even declared Petros the pelican their mascot.

Nature's Spectacle **141**

Europe's Coolest Little Hot Spot

It was a cool summer afternoon as we made our way east along the Ring Road to a glacier whose name is, quite simply, unpronounceable. Following a short trek over the sharp and broken lava rock, our guide began to explain a bit of the glacial history of Iceland as he helped me strap on my crampons. After several days mixing sightseeing with gourmet dining, rafting, and light adventure with a small group of fellow outdoor enthusiasts, this was the experience I had been waiting for since arriving on the remote North Atlantic island.

It wasn't long before the sun stopped flirting with the clouds and the cool breeze turned into a startlingly bitter wind, followed by a brief blast of arctic snow. While the average temperature in Reykjavik during Iceland's warmest month is 15° C (59° F), for a few short minutes, I felt like a polar explorer on an uncharted expedition as we walked in single file, avoiding the bottomless crevasses. Moments later, our sudden and dramatic taste

of an Icelandic winter passed and our arctic adventure turned back into a comfortable, crunchy stroll over the ancient lava-stained ice flow.

While its name would lead you to believe that the entire island is one solid block of ice, actually only ten percent of Iceland is covered in glaciers, and they are melting fast. The glaciers we visit today are the remnants of icecaps formed during the "Little Ice Age" between 1500 and 1900 CE and have shown a steady retreat over the past eighty years. In fact, the Sólheimajökull outlet glacier of the Myrdalsjökull icecap in the far south of the island where I was trekking is currently receding at a rate of about 300 feet (91 m) per year.

In a coincidence of nature, Iceland is also wrapped in the warm embrace of the Gulf Stream, which brings it a surprisingly moderate and livable climate despite its proximity to the Arctic Circle. When the long winter nights yield to the endless days of sunlight in June, the countryside awakens to a welcomed lushness and an increasing number of tourists. But to truly appreciate this beautiful island, you need to understand that ice is only half of the story.

Born of a geothermal hot spot straddling the mid-Atlantic ridge, where tectonic plates are tearing at the edges of continents, the rugged beauty of Iceland is evidence of a living planet. Primitive forces of nature have spewed, cut, torn, and ripped the earth to create a land of extremes constantly being shaped and altered by volcanic activity and glacial ice. The raw and unbridled landscape is dotted by moss-covered rocks from ancient lava flows, active geysers, massive glaciers, volcanoes, steaming lava fields, hot springs, stunning fjords, and swirling glacial rivers that drop over spectacular waterfalls.

Belonging to both North America and Europe, Iceland is geologically one of the youngest landmasses in the world and is literally being pulled apart as the two continents separate by several centimeters each year and new earth is created from below. This slow and sometimes violent struggle has left a volcanic belt of activity in its wake and a dramatic scar across the entire island from the southwest to the northeast.

At the Silfra Rift in the National Park Thingvellir, the crack between continents can also be experienced under water. In a truly one-of-a-kind snorkeling adventure, our group donned dry-suits before stepping off the Silfra platform into the thirty-four-degree, crystal-clear glacial water flowing into Thingvellir Lake. The visibility was stunning as a mild current started us drifting through a narrow canyon in a vast lava field, which ended as the crack feathered out at the edge of the lake surrounded by spectacular snow-capped volcanic peaks.

THE GREATEST SHOW ON EARTH

The day begins early in East Africa. At the first light of dawn in Kenya's Maasai Mara National Reserve, safari trucks speed off into the sunrise in hopes of a close encounter with one of Africa's glamorous cats. The early morning is the best time to catch a glimpse of the beautiful and elusive animals before they seek shelter from the midday heat. While lions, leopards, and cheetahs are thrilling to see in the wild, offering the sexiest photographic memories, it is the strange-looking and ungainly wildebeest that offers one of the greatest natural spectacles on earth.

The wildebeest, or gnu (pronounced g-noo or new), is a bovid antelope belonging to the family of even-toed, horned ungulates that includes cattle and goats. With its shaggy mane, long, thin face, pointed beard, and spindly legs, the wildebeest is immediately recognizable on the Serengeti plains. It is also quite possibly the single most important species in the Serengeti-Mara ecosystem.

From their historic breeding grounds in Tanzania's Ngorongoro Conservation Area to their long grazing layover in the Mara, each year

an estimated 1.5 million wildebeest, along with hundreds of thousands of zebra and gazelle, make a 500-mile (804-km) migratory circle in search of food. They are constantly on the move, devouring thousands of acres of grassland before continuing on to greener pastures.

While they do have distinctive family groupings within the herds, wildebeest travel as a giant swarm. Over the course of the migration, they experience the full cycle of life as they run a gauntlet of never-ending dangers. During a six-week period in February and March, nearly a half-million calves are born. Remarkably, nearly 80 percent are born during the same two weeks. Within minutes, a newborn calf can stand and then run with the herd. Drawn by thunder or the smell of distant rains, huge numbers soon spread out over Tanzania's southwest plains, enjoying nutrient-rich grass and abundant water.

The vast open grasslands of the Serengeti contain the largest concentration of wildlife on earth. Millions of years ago, the volcanoes of the Great Rift Valley laid down a blanket of ash that hardened like concrete and created a shallow fertile soil virtually impenetrable to the roots of large trees. The massive caldera of Tanzania's Ngorongoro Crater is a remnant of one of these giant volcanoes that exploded and collapsed on itself two or three million years ago. One of the few trees that has thrived in the unique soil is the acacia, which dot the barren landscape.

WHEN THE SHORT GRAZES ARE exhausted in the south and the dry season begins, the migration starts north toward the Grumeti River for mating season. In late May to early June, wildebeest begin their rut, as males battle over females. By July, the migration begins its turn northeast for the Maasai Mara, where they will graze until October before returning south to their breeding grounds in Tanzania—with pregnant females leading the way.

By the time we arrived in the Maasai Mara after first spending a few days at the Samburu Game Reserve and Lake Nakuru, it was mid-October. The feasting was nearly over, and rains were threatening on the horizon. Thousands of animals had already started their migration south, and the rest were forming into single-file lines stretching for miles across the border into Tanzania. All over the Mara these lines were converging around corners and over hills. We encountered huge pockets of wildebeest apparently reluctant to leave—only the last few stragglers remained north of the Mara River.

I have made several trips to the Maasai Mara, but this was the first time I had seen the great herds on their annual journey. It is actually a relatively new phenomenon to witness the migration in the Maasai Mara at all. In fact, it has been only in my lifetime that the migration has spilled across the Mara River and into Kenya. Disease, human encroachment, and shifting rain patterns in the Serengeti-Mara ecosystem have combined over the last forty years to change the survival equation for the great herds on the grasslands of East Africa.

During the first half of the twentieth century, the wildebeest population (along with the African buffalo) was devastated by rinderpest, a highly contagious virus that is thought to have been introduced to East Africa by domestic cattle. In the 1950s, a broad-scale program was initiated to eradicate the virus, and, in 1962, the last case of rinderpest was found in wildebeest. From a population of 250,000 in 1961, the number of wildebeest swelled to nearly 1.5 million by 1978 and has remained stable ever since.

The other contributing factor to the adjusted migration route and rapid population growth was a significant change in rainfall patterns that brought increased precipitation to the northern Serengeti-Mara region during the dry season. With a healthy population and increased supply of reliable food just to the north, the wildebeest would thrive for decades and affect the lives of countless other animals. At a time when human population growth threatened animal habitats all over the world, the wildebeest extended its range and helped to sustain the big cats of East Africa.

FOLLOWING LUNCH AND A BRIEF SIESTA, we boarded our safari truck for an afternoon game drive. In a routine that had developed after days on safari together, we found our respective positions in the truck, readied our cameras, and started peppering our Kikuyu guide Peter Muigai Muruthi with dozens of questions about what we were seeing through the dusty windows of our Land Cruiser.

Thirty minutes out, we slowly pulled into a clearing along the Mara River where Muigai shut off the rumbling diesel engine, revealing the soundtrack of East Africa we had come to appreciate. The afternoon wind on the grasses, the distant songs of exotic birds, the rush of the nearby river, and the increasingly familiar grunts, growls, and snorts of the world's greatest animal sanctuary had become an enjoyable and familiar part of our safari experience.

At first glance, it was quiet along the river. We spotted a group of four zebra walking toward the water as we positioned our bean bags on the rim of the roof hatch to support our long camera lenses. Several other safari trucks were now beginning to gather along both sides of the river. Suddenly, it felt like something was about to happen…and soon. Previously hidden among the rocks and trees above the zebra, hundreds of wildebeest emerged and nervously assembled along the steep bank.

As our excitement grew, a fifth zebra joined the others carefully sipping water at the riverbank. Skittish by nature, zebra will often take a quick drink of water before jumping back from some unseen danger, repeating the process until they have had their fill. But when Muigai broke the silence in his commanding baritone voice with the single word "crocodile!" it was clear that these zebra had something to fear.

Coming around the corner of a small peninsula, we could see a long wake moving quickly through the water. We barely had time to focus our cameras when the massive 18-foot crocodile sprang from the river at the unsuspecting zebra. They jumped with incredible agility and scampered away unharmed. Adrenaline rushed through us as we checked our cameras to see if we had captured the moment—it happened so fast.

As we began to relax and catch our breath, a single wildebeest entered the water. Cries of "Oh no! Oh no!" came from the front of our truck as the anticipation of what might happen gripped us. The croc was slow to react. As the wildebeest exited the river safely on the other side, two others began their crossing. A nearby pod of hippopotamuses started grunting loudly in a chilling chorus of understanding—they knew what was coming next. Seconds later, ten more wildebeest, then twenty, then hundreds, jumped into the water in a disorderly mass. Through the dust and chaos, we lost sight of the crocodile. For a few brief minutes, the river was overwhelmed with fearless beasts frantically swimming to safety—and then…it was over. The heart-pounding drama gave way to an orderly walk toward the rest of the migrating herd.

We stood speechless for several minutes as quiet returned to the Mara, and we noticed the zebra were still on the far side of the river. Their simple quest for water erupted suddenly into a brief but wild frenzy. After the dust had settled, we thanked Muigai for putting us in the right place at the right time to experience one of the most dramatic scenes in the greatest show on earth. He responded with a characteristically humble "You're welcome" as he fired up the engine and led us away from the river in search of Africa's glamorous cats. We did soon encounter a resting cheetah that posed patiently for us in the fading afternoon sun, but on this trip, it was the strange-looking and ungainly gnu that created the memory we will cherish for a lifetime.

Greenland's Icy Lure

Fog rolled quickly up the fjord, enveloping us in a colorless milieu with no visible boundary separating the perfectly still water from the cold wet air. Small surface ripples created by our zodiac boat were the only indication that we were, in fact, moving. Our driver carefully navigated around massive chunks of arctic ice that suddenly appeared and disappeared like an enchanted mirage on the grey, featureless horizon. The baritone growl of the motor echoed off the surrounding granite walls as horns and whistles announced from the distance that we were not alone.

For two days we had waited for the wind and rain to subside before traveling down Tunulliarfik Fjord to our remote tent camp at Qaleraliq Glacier. Our guide Pedro casually noted that the dense fog can last for several days in South Greenland, but it was the high winds that made travel through the fjords particularly dangerous. As our speed increased, eleven of us huddled together around the outside of the zodiac, wrapped in thick parkas, peering out of small openings in our protective hoods to catch a fleeting glimpse of a passing iceberg.

After a forty-five-minute, adrenaline-fueled arctic boat ride, we pulled into the small harbor at Narsaq. Low-lying clouds shrouded the twin

peaks that frame the third most-populated town in South Greenland. The iconic, brightly painted cottages were quiet as a soft rain began to fall. Our stop was brief. We boarded a smaller boat with a mountain guide equipped with crampons, helmets, harnesses, and ice axes. Before settling into our camp, we would be trekking across one of the oldest and largest masses of ice on the planet.

Recently, this mass of ice has inspired a flood of climate scientists, researchers, and historians onto the ancient ice sheet to sample ice-cores and document the thickness and movement of dozens of individual glaciers. In their quest to understand the causes and effects of climatic fluctuations, many scientists believe that what happens in Greenland over the next couple of decades will answer important questions about the complex interactions between our atmosphere and the world's great oceans.

These scientists and researchers are no longer alone in their exploration of one of the world's most remote and visually stunning destinations. Adventure travelers and hearty tourists from around the globe have also been lured to this icy world by spectacular images of a truly wild place. I joined travelers from Germany, Spain, France, Australia, South Africa, Greece, Ireland, England, and the United States to experience a landscape that has become the focus of an often intense and politically charged global warming debate.

As the boat carrying our group motored along the glacier front toward our landing, the enormity of the massive ice wall left us speechless. We disembarked onto huge flat rocks and scrambled up giant boulders to the base of the glacier where we geared up for the trek. We followed our guide in single file, passing holes, drains, caves, seracs, and crevasses until we reached a vertical wall of translucent ice already affixed with ropes to belay our climb to another, higher level of the glacier. The persistent overcast sky and low-lying clouds unfortunately prevented a view of the vast inland glacier, but our intimacy with the impressive ice formations hinted at the incredible scale of the ice sheet beyond.

When we finally reached camp, we found a warm meal waiting for us in the dining tent. Other groups were already settled in and invited us to join them at large picnic-style tables. Clothing hung from the tent walls, and several people gathered around a small space heater to dry their boots. The wet and exhausted tourist-adventurers who surrounded me shared stories, experiences, and laughter.

AFTER SEVERAL DAYS OF OVERCAST, when the skies finally cleared and the fog lifted, the unmatched beauty of the landscape was revealed. From a small bluff near camp, we could see for the first time that the three visible glacier fronts were actually one massive flow of ice with three separate routes to the fjord. As the sun dipped toward the horizon, deep shadows and pockets of iridescent blue created a three-dimensional glacial panorama. Soon the magnificent colors of sunset reflected in the fjord as our camp drifted into a perpetual twilight. The silence of the arctic night was interrupted only by the eerie rumble of moving ice.

The next morning greeted us with a spectacular sunrise and brilliant blue skies. We walked along the sandy shore before boarding our zodiac for the ride back to our base at the fjordside village of Qassiarsuk. We were excited and renewed by the sunshine as we once again entered the harbor at Narsaq. This time the town was bustling with activity. Fishermen packed their boats as children walked like mini glacier trekkers in single file on their way to school. We had an hour to wander through town and photograph the colorful cottages against the backdrop of blue skies and glowing white towers of ice.

With a total population of only around fifty-seven thousand, Greenland is the least densely populated country on earth. Most Greenlanders are decendants of Inuit and eighteenth-century Danish colonists and live along the habitable fringe between the ice and the sea. Over one-quarter of the country's population lives in Greenland's capital, Nuuk. The rest live in a handful of small towns along the west coast, separated by a deeply indented coastline that makes road development between towns impossible.

There is very little remaining of the Viking presence on Greenland, except for a few scattered ruins and the legends passed down in Norse sagas. By the year 874 CE, colonists

from Norway had settled permanently in Iceland, bringing with them a dairy-based economy that they soon combined with seal hunting and fishing to earn a living in the new land. Warm summers allowed ample hay and barley harvests for winter food and fodder. They were successful and thrived at the edge of the arctic.

The Norse were essentially farmers and fishermen who did a bit of plundering and pillaging along the way. One of those tough seafaring farmers, the infamous Erik the Red, sailed west out of Iceland after being banished from the island for three years for murder. He set off into unknown waters with a small group of men to explore reports of mysterious islands sighted by one of his relatives some half-century earlier. He landed on the rugged eastern shore of Greenland in 982 but soon sailed around the southern tip to a fjord near Qaqortog. He spent the next three years exploring the fjords of the south.

There is evidence that Erik the Red landed on Greenland during a period of exceptional warmth and stability known as the Medieval Warm Period. In the southwestern corner of the island, the Norseman found green summer pastures that provided grazing land for sheep, abundant fish, and large numbers of sea mammals. Erik returned to Iceland with glowing reports about the fertile land he called Greenland, which he thought would be an attractive name to lure potential settlers.

A year later, Erik and fourteen ships arrived on Greenland to establish settlements in the sheltered waters of the southwest. Eventually, four thousand Norse settled the massive island, raising sheep and cattle like they did back home. They built churches, homes, farms, and communities on relatively fertile ground, compared to the thin volcanic soil and hardscrabble of Iceland. Erik himself settled in the heart of the richest farmland at a place that is now the village of Qassiarsuk.

WE WERE GREETED AT QASSIARSUK BY several staff of the Leif Erickson Hostel and by its Spanish owner, polar explorer Ramon Larramendi. Larramendi became a legend of sorts following his three-year arctic expedition from Greenland to Alaska by foot, kayak, and dog sled in the early 1990s. The hostel has become his home in Greenland and a support enclave for the kayak expeditions he leads throughout the country.

After Ramon welcomed us to the hostel, Pedro took us on a tour of the village and the ruins of Brattahild—the name of Erik the Red's original farmstead. The modern village dates from a successful effort to reintroduce sheep breeding to the area in the 1920s and is home to about sixty year-round residents. The highlights of the tour were the picturesque re-creation of what archaeologists believe was the first church built in the New World and a turf-covered reconstruction of a Norse longhouse.

There are many theories about why the Norse mysteriously disappeared from Greenland after over four centuries of settlement. Perhaps a massive epidemic swept the island or a blight devastated their grazing land. But one contributing factor to the Norse exodus was most likely the onset of a five-hundred-year period known as the Little Ice Age. By 1300, Greenland was already experiencing increasing cold and drastic, unpredictable shifts in weather. Glacial advances began in the early thirteenth century and increased the ice pack, while stormy seas in the northernmost Atlantic disrupted critical trading routes. What we do know is that the last known written record of the Norse on Greenland wasn't about a war, plague, or famine; it was about a wedding in 1408 at Hvalsey Church near Qaqortoq.

By 1300, the Norse had also been sharing their remote island with Inuit, who arrived from northern Canada centuries earlier. While they brought with them dogsleds, kayaks, and other essential tools and skills that would help them survive the Little Ice Age, the Norse still relied on the same fishing and dairy economy introduced during the time of Erik the Red. Their existence depended on storing enough hay and fish to survive the long, harsh winter. Even a small shift in the growing season would have caused livestock to die and put vulnerable settlers at risk.

Nobody knows if the current weather patterns will lead to another ice age or if we are heading into a prolonged warming period like the one that allowed the Norse to thrive, but the history of Greenland is a history of survival and adaptation in extreme arctic conditions. It is a challenging and unforgiving land of amazing beauty, where life clings to the fertile fringes between the ice and the sea.

OPPOSITE PAGE: Cumberland Falls, Kentucky, USA

Chapter 7
The Adventure Begins

ad·ven·ture *noun* \əd-ˈven-chər\
: an exciting or remarkable experience usually involving danger and unknown risks

One of the fastest-growing trends in travel is active and adventure tourism, but defining exactly what adventure travel means can be a little tricky. For some, an adventure could simply mean being outside of their comfort zone on a cultural safari. For others, it might entail climbing, rafting, jumping, biking, or diving. It is a fact that some of the world's most spectacular landscapes and remote vistas are not easy to get to. Many can be reached only by foot, horse, canoe, raft, or kayak. Adding a sense of danger or stepping into the unknown, even for a brief time, can be a stimulating experience.

A growing number of travelers are seeking a different kind of vacation by climbing mountains, running rapids, or learning scuba to explore the underwater world. Just because you aren't an experienced outdoor enthusiast doesn't mean you can't participate in an adventure. There are many opportunities that allow you to learn a new skill from professional instructors right at your destination; kayaking, rock climbing, surfing, snorkeling, and diving are just a few. Tour operators are also adding hiking, biking, and rafting components to add an active and adventurous edge to an otherwise typical sightseeing tour. Most importantly, be honest with yourself about your capabilities and limitations.

BELOW: Mount Kilimanjaro, Tanzania
OPPOSITE PAGE: Saint Martin

Getting There

Deciding which adventure holiday is right for you can be an intimidating experience. Adventure tours are often defined as "hard" or "soft." Hard adventures may require you to be in top physical condition, like high-altitude trekking in the Himalaya, climbing Mount Kilimanjaro, and extensive biking tours or kayaking trips. Other adventure tours can incorporate thrilling activities, like river rafting, dog sledding, or a walking safari on the African plains, which don't require the same level of fitness but are still active.

Obviously for a photographer, traveling to a place that only a few people have ever seen is a rewarding experience both photographically and emotionally. Some places are so beautiful that it is hard to take a bad photograph. The hardest part is just getting there with your camera. There are also numerous new challenges, from dealing with extreme weather to practical considerations about protecting and carrying your equipment.

My "kit" of photographic equipment changes depending upon the challenges of weather and limitations of weight. Weight is an important consideration when flying on small bush planes or helicopters and when you are hauling your gear on your back. Many internal flights in remote areas of the world have weight limitations, not just for your equipment but for everything you are bringing. And, while you might not mind lugging a heavy backpack up a mountain, most reputable tour operators place a weight limit on what they allow their porters to carry for you.

Do you really need a backup camera body, an extra lens, a tripod, or a laptop computer? In the modern digital world, another major consideration is whether there will be electricity along your route. If you are on a daytrip or short adventure, it might not matter, but if you are going someplace remote for an extended period of time, preparing for electrical needs is a priority. Should you bring multiple camera batteries? Can you make it through the trip with just your supply of memory cards, or will you need to download to a storage device?

A Watery World

Water is a natural enemy of electronic equipment. Many cameras are splash proof, but if you are working around or in water, it pays to be extra careful. I have often approached kayaking and rafting much like snorkeling and diving. Even on a sunny day kayaking on flat water, I assume that my camera will get wet (yes, I have flipped a kayak with an expensive camera and lens in my lap…lesson learned).

Over the years, I have used underwater cameras like the Nikonos V for film, various camera housings, and a modern waterproof digital point-and-shoot to photograph kayaking and rafting adventures. I also almost always pack my good DSLR and a telephoto zoom in a dry bag to use on the shore or when we are in calm water. While the kayak or raft is your transportation to some remote and beautiful locations, part of the experience is to also capture action shots of the adventure. Since the kayak sits just inches above the water, photographing other kayakers or including the front of your boat in a shot of a scenic background can give a sense of place, movement, and excitement.

If you are rafting white water, the action shot to get, of course, is the running of rapids. Even if you have a waterproof camera, it is very difficult

A Matter of Perspective

We are visual creatures who comprehend the world by interpreting what we see. We not only recognize the content in most photographs, we intuitively understand structural components like perspective and depth of field. To our eye, objects that are closer to us appear larger than objects farther away. We know that the tree off in the distance is larger than it appears on the horizon. Human beings also have stereoscopic vision, which allows us to gauge distance and navigate through a three-dimensional world.

In a two-dimensional photograph, we gauge distance and our place in that world through perspective. Perspective is composed of visual clues that add depth and dimension to a photograph. Foreground objects that appear closer to the camera establish our location and guide the eye through the image into the distance. Just like a road or landscape that vanishes in the distance is perspective, so, too, is the convergence of a building as we look up toward the sky. We intuitively know we are looking up.

to shoot as you are going through a rapid. Big rapids will require everyone onboard to paddle hard to control the raft, and a giant wave of water can make for an unexpected swim. A good way to get action shots is to ask your guide to run the rapid first. Often, there will be calm water below the rapid or an eddy (the space on the downstream side of an object, like a large boulder or outcropping, that is devoid of current) to shoot from as the others come through the rapid.

Let your guide know that you want to create action shots on your rafting trip. You might also be able to exit the raft and scurry down the shoreline a short distance to photograph your group going through a stretch of rapids, and re-enter the boat a bit farther down river. Your guide will know the best place to do this, so ask before the trip begins and he can plan for it. If you are stuck in the raft, sitting in the back and photographing through other rafters, using them as foreground framing, is a wonderful technique for a "you are there" feeling.

Peeking Below the Waves

Where there is water and something to look at below the surface, you will find snorkeling and diving opportunities. The underwater world is a true mystery to most of us and a source of fear and fascination. Snorkeling is pretty easy to learn and requires no special training. You put on a mask with a snorkel and fins and swim around on the surface of the water. Many waterproof digital point-and-shoot cameras, or even the disposable cameras purchased at the dive shop, can make wonderful shots around coral reefs and small schools of fish near rocky shorelines.

Since you are shooting in shallow water, visibility is usually not a problem. Colors are often bright on a sunny day. As you go deeper, the properties of water and its effect on light add photographic challenges. Water is approximately eight hundred times denser than air and absorbs light one wavelength at a time. Red and orange are absorbed first, often within fifteen to twenty feet (four to six meters), followed by yellow and green. To capture good underwater

OPPOSITE PAGE LEFT TO RIGHT: Kentucky, USA; Iceland
BELOW: Dominica

Vanishing Point

All perspective photographs have a horizon line that represents objects in the distance. The horizon line might be visible, as in a landscape photograph, or implied by a "vanishing point," where all lines parallel to the viewer's line of sight recede to a point on the horizon. Think of the classic railroad tracks vanishing at a point in the distance. An angled horizon or unfamiliar perspective can create the sense of movement or tension in an image.

images, photographers need to compensate for this color loss as they go deeper. Color compensating filters are an option for some professionals under controlled circumstances, but they increase exposure times, thus raising the ISO and/or slowing the shutter speed. The easiest way to shoot underwater is to get close to your subject and use a flash.

Not only is color lost going deeper, it is lost horizontally as well. Objects farther away from the camera will appear as colorless shadows in the distance. Even with a flash, you must get close to your subject. Any particles in the water will create tiny white specs when illuminated by the flash. Besides using a flash, another useful technique is to shoot pointing up toward the surface to add depth to a foreground subject.

Scuba diving clearly requires special training, and good underwater photography is a skill mastered by very few. I wouldn't call myself

BELOW LEFT TO RIGHT: Yucatan, Mexico; Iceland

an expert diver by any stretch. Officially I am a Scuba Schools International (SSI) level 3 diver with almost forty logged dives. I don't shoot underwater professionally. I don't plan vacations around diving or haul my gear around the world, but if you are a diver and travel to some great dive locations, you try to go diving. I most often rent a camera with a flash from the dive operator and shoot on automatic. I am a dive tourist.

Going to Extremes

There are a lot of reasons why individuals seek an experience in the outdoors. The most obvious are to briefly escape our daily lives, to relieve a little stress, to be with friends, or simply to have some fun and get a little exercise. There is, however, a group of people who engage in self-propelled adventures to challenge themselves against the extremes. While I have always considered myself to be in the "have fun and get a little exercise" category, I have found myself working in some extreme environments.

The challenges shooting in extreme conditions, such as heat, cold, and altitude, are more about the functioning of our bodies than the functioning of the camera. Human beings are not built for extremes, but modern digital cameras usually work just fine in such conditions. The biggest problem is often the batteries, which need to be kept warm and will lose their

OPPOSITE PAGE LEFT TO RIGHT: Inca Trail, Peru; Kentucky, USA
BELOW: Taklamakan Desert, China

Human beings are not built for extremes, but modern digital cameras usually work just fine in such conditions.

charge very quickly when the temperatures dip far below freezing. I keep batteries in a small bag close to my body with a silica packet or two to help absorb any condensation that may form. I only insert the batteries into my cameras just before shooting.

We all know that when we come in from the cold, glasses will fog up almost immediately. Camera lenses fog up, too, and if there is any microscopic space where air can get between elements, condensation on the inside of your glass can leave water rings as it evaporates. Large temperature swings can also damage the computer and inner workings of your camera. A tip is to seal your cameras and lenses in ziplock bags with the outside cold air, which will let them slowly warm up to room temperature when you come inside or back onto a heated tour bus. If there is any condensation inside your camera and you return to the extreme cold, it is likely to freeze.

Likewise, heat can also do damage to your camera sensor and the lubrication in your zoom lens. Nothing good happens inside your camera as the temperature soars over 100 degrees Fahrenheit. Blowing sand or fine dust is another extreme danger to your camera. Never change a lens or memory card in windy, sandy conditions. This will help keep your sensor clean, but even a few grains of sand can do a lot of damage to the delicate insides of a DSLR. If you know you will be in desert conditions, use a clear or UV filter to protect your lens or even consider bringing along your underwater housing if you have it.

The Adventure Begins **169**

FIELD NOTES

Alaska Cruise Adventure

We were traveling a bit farther into the mountains than usual, noted our young pilot as we rose higher and higher into the brilliant blue Alaskan sky. For nearly twenty minutes, we slowly and deliberately climbed above the stunning snow-capped mountains north of Juneau. The impressive Mendenhall Glacier looked like a twisting mountain highway out of the small, tinted windows of our able little helicopter.

I listened intently to his commentary as we navigated through the turbulence and shifting currents created by the massive peaks. After one final burst of power to clear a jagged ridge, we began our descent toward Gilkey Glacier and the ice-trekking experience that I had been looking forward to for months. I attempted to capture a few snapshots of the spectacular landscape, when Barbara's sudden and intense grasp of my left thigh reminded me that I wasn't alone on my great Alaskan adventure.

While Barbara and I have been a couple for almost thirty years, it didn't take us nearly that long to figure out that our definitions of vacation are very different. Barbara can relax at a beach or lakeside for days—I can't! Over the years, I have been only marginally successful at talking her into joining me on some new experiences that fall well outside her ideal vacation scenario. So when I suggested that she join me for an assignment aboard Holland America's *ms Oosterdam* on an Inside Passage cruise to Alaska, there was no lengthy negotiation, no pleading, no expensive bottles of wine—just an immediate and enthusiastic, "I'm in!"

As we reviewed our cruise literature, one particular shore excursion ignited my passion, a flightseeing and glacier trek out of our first port of call in Juneau. Within minutes of our gentle landing on the centuries-old ice flow, we were outfitted with crampons and helmets and given a brief lesson on the proper use of our ice axe before setting out on our two-hour trek. Barbara had an unsettling look of intensity on her face as she took her first tentative steps on the unfamiliar surface. Following our guides, we carefully made our way along the glacier's edge and over the occasional small crevasse created by the melting ice of early summer. We soon began to appreciate that we were sharing an amazing experience in a place where very few people have ever walked.

We arrived back in Juneau with plenty of time to enjoy a wonderful meal of fish and chips and start the shopping portion of our adventure. The eclectic shops provided a great opportunity for Barbara to enjoy a bit of "alone time" while I headed to the famous Red Dog Saloon to share stories of adventure and bond with other intrepid cruisers before heading back to the ship.

As we made the long approach to Hubbard Glacier, one of the last highlights of the cruise, Barbara and I crowded with new friends at the bow of the ship and shared a true sense of amazement at Alaska's impressive coastline. With the glacier as our background, the engines were cut and we drifted in the bay while we enjoyed a grilled salmon lunch at the Lido deck pool. There is simply no experience quite like it in the world.

FIELD NOTES

Midnight Accent

I didn't need a wakeup call. I could hear Jeffery, our cook, preparing a late night meal of porridge and popcorn just before midnight. I hadn't slept much since lying down in my tent at 5:30 p.m., so I was thrilled to hear the familiar popping sound to relieve me of my restless night. After a few last-minute clothing decisions, I gathered my trekking poles and pack and joined my guide, Goodluck Kiget, in our meal tent. We didn't talk much and we didn't need to. The time had finally come to climb the last 4,000 feet (1,219 m) to the summit of Mount Kilimanjaro.

It was warmer than expected as we set off into the darkness. As we approached the trailhead, I could see a line of small white dots snaking almost vertically up the mountain. It wasn't long before the exertion forced me to drop a layer of clothing. Hour after hour we walked, rarely looking past the small pool of light cast by our headlamps. The only sound was the crunching of rocks under my feet and the rhythmic tapping of my trekking poles. We stopped along the trail only occasionally to hydrate and grab a quick snack. We made good time as we went higher into the night. Too good, as it would later turn out.

While Kilimanjaro is easily accessible and doesn't require any technical climbing skills other than grit, it is also the most underestimated mountain in the world. With Uhuru Peak reaching 19,341 feet (5,895 m) above the plains of Africa, it is the world's highest freestanding mountain. Between fifteen thousand and twenty thousand people make the attempt to summit the often-called "everyman's Everest" each year, with only around 50 percent actually reaching their goal. The success rates vary greatly. While an estimated 30 percent of climbers summit on five-day routes, nearly 85 percent reach the top on an eight-day route, which is less strenuous and allows the body additional time to acclimatize.

I was doing a six-day trek on the Machame route and our pace was fast. We broke down camp early each morning in glorious sunshine with stunning views. Our goal was to make it to our next destination camp before the inevitable afternoon rains. By the time we reached Barranco Wall and the push toward high camp, I had my trail legs and felt strong, with no ill effects from the altitude. But there were many slow and methodical steps yet to be made.

The mist and fog rolled in over the huge boulders sheltering the assorted colors of tents haphazardly erected in small clusters at Barfu Camp. Other groups of trekkers were breaking down after summiting a few hours before we arrived from Barranco. We waited patiently for our chosen spot to be vacated as the rains descended upon the mountaintop. We were offered no hint, no glimpse of the peak we would soon ascend.

We reached Stella Point at 5:00 a.m. Stella Point is a big milestone on the approach to the summit and a popular place for trekkers to stop and watch the sunrise. But sunrise was still an hour away, so we decided to push on in the cold and dark. As we got closer and closer to Uhuru Peak, every step took effort. Small groups passed us on their way down, and I could see a stationary gathering of lights in the distance.

We arrived at 5:45 a.m., which was, unfortunately, nearly a half hour before the first light of the sun would rise over the plains of Tanzania. The cold on the summit was excruciating. I unpacked my equipment with the light of my headlamp and stood patiently in the darkness. I warmed quickly when the first light of day finally peeked between the clouds below us and focused my camera on the unrivaled beauty from the roof of Africa.

THE EVEREST HIGHWAY

We started hearing our first reports in Namche Bazaar. The news wasn't promising. Heavy snow had temporarily closed Cho La Pass. For almost a week as we journeyed higher into the mountains, the thought of a dangerous ten-hour trek over a snow-covered pass in the Himalaya lingered unspoken as we gathered around dung-fueled stoves in our nightly teahouse sanctuaries. The pass is the shortcut to Everest Base Camp (EBC) across the saddle between the Gokyo and Khumbu valleys, and it was where we were heading.

I sat quietly with the small group of Americans I had joined on the trail in Namche, as two young German men shared the tale of their crossing. They had just come through the pass from the opposite direction and told of a treacherous descent on an obscured and slippery trail. "It was brutal," one commented in accented English, as he told of a biting wind and fierce cold that swallowed them from behind just before noon. "It started as a gentle fog," he continued, but it soon turned into a "swirling snowstorm," reducing their visibility to less than thirty feet (ten meters) and covering the trace that marked the trail.

The Germans had trekked from east to west after visiting EBC. It was early May, the beginning of summit season on the mountain. Hundreds

of climbers from around the world, and hundreds more Sherpa and porters, would be assembling in the transitory outpost at the base of Khumbu Glacier. Each year in May, a brief weather window opens and the skies clear just enough to allow climbers a fleeting opportunity to summit what the Sherpa call Chomolungma, "The Goddess Mother of the World." It is also a time when thousands of tourist trekkers share the trail to EBC and enjoy the calm alpine weather before the monsoons arrive in June.

After hearing their story, we huddled around the stove for a group meeting with our guide Amber. The question that confronted us was whether to chance Cho La Pass, or walk down 5,250 feet (1,600 m) the way we came up, and then climb back up another 5,250 feet on the Everest Base Camp Trail. Cho La Pass is one of the marquee achievements on the Everest trekking circuit. It is a 17,590-foot-high (5,361-m) rite of passage for high-altitude trekkers. On this trip, it was my summit, my "Everest," and I wanted it!

We knew people were crossing through the pass despite the conditions, but we also knew that the helicopters we saw flying up and down the valley every morning were evacuating tourist trekkers who found themselves in trouble. Since we would be traveling in the opposite direction from the Germans, crossing the pass would mean a long, steep climb up a snow-covered ridge into oncoming weather.

It is easy to underestimate the power of nature and how quickly the weather can change in the mountains. Every day on the trail, I witnessed the stunning panorama of jagged white spires piercing the fluorescent blue sky vanish into whiteness as the fog and snow descended from the east. Did I feel lucky that somehow tomorrow would be different? People die in these mountains because of pride and stubbornness. They go up when they should go down.

Once the decision was made, I felt a sense of relief. The next morning we left Gokyo and retraced our tracks past the small villages of Machhermo and Dole. The trek down gave me strength as we descended into the valley. Since we were acclimatized to over 16,500 feet (5,029 m), we would go fast up the trail to Everest Base Camp.

I COULD SEE AN ELDERLY MAN out the window chopping wood in the distance as I snuggled closer to the warm stove at the trekkers lodge at Phortse. We arrived just as the first drops of heavy wet snow foreshadowed the predictable afternoon weather. Phortse is a small village with a scattering of lodges sprinkled among brick homes and fenced pastureland. Before foreigners started coming to the region in the 1950s, Phortse was the highest inhabited village. Locals used only the grassy areas at the base of the mountains as summer grazing lands. The lonely clusters of buildings nestled amidst the peaks, like Dole and Machhermo, hadn't existed.

Before 1950, attempts to conquer Everest were launched from Tibet on the northern

The Everest Highway

route to the summit discovered by English mountaineer George Mallory in the 1920s. Nepal was a mysterious and isolated land that very few westerners had ever seen. But that changed quickly in the first few years of the century's middle decade as the newly formed People's Republic of China invaded Tibet, effectively shutting off the northern route.

Almost immediately, the French, British, Austrians, Swiss, and Japanese sent mountaineering expeditions to Nepal, unleashing what would come to be called the "golden decade" of Himalayan mountaineering. The people who grazed their yaks, goats, and sheep in these mountains started building permanent structures and began servicing the waves of mountaineers who were using the old trails to explore northern Nepal and climb her lofty peaks. They started with small shelters, which grew over the years into today's "teahouse" treks and full-service accommodations.

The teahouses along the trails are simple, and very little effort has gone into making them comfortable. Rooms are typically constructed with thin plywood walls and contain a cot or two. There is often no electricity, and the shared toilet is a porcelain-framed hole in the ground with an adjacent bucket of water for flushing. A shower is a rare indulgence. Most have one main dining and gathering room with a small stove to provide evening warmth for guests. At night, our porters would sleep in this crowded but warm space as we retired to our frigid plywood boxes.

From the gateway town of Lukla to EBC, trekkers will climb a little over 8,300 feet (2,540 m). What makes this a slow journey of many days is not the difficulty of the trail, but the daily altitude gain. Typically, trekkers ascend no more than 1,000–1,300 feet (300–400 m) a day as they acclimatize and their blood begins to make more red blood cells, carrying more oxygen to vital organs. Going too high too fast can lead to acute mountain sickness, or worse—an emergency helicopter evacuation. Teahouses have popped up every few kilometers, so trekkers are rarely more than a couple hours walk from shelter.

With no such elevation restrictions, Amber and I pushed hard up the trail, stopping only briefly at Pangboche to visit the oldest monastery in the Khumbu. Most climbers stop at either this monastery or the monastery at Tengboche for a blessing on their way to EBC. As we entered the four hundred-year-old building, we could hear the drums and temple bells of the local monks. We removed our shoes and entered the prayer room. The walls were lined with Buddhist shrines draped with hundreds of white scarves known as *kata*. Murals framed the windows where the monks sat before tables, chanting and sipping yak-butter tea. Ceremonial masks and beautifully painted *thangka* hung from the wooden rafters, while along the back wall, butter candles illuminated the offerings of pilgrims, trekkers, and climbers.

LEAVING PANGBOCHE, WE CLIMBED QUICKLY past Pheriche through fog and snow before stopping at Dughla. When we arrived, the main room was already filled with two dozen porters, Sherpa, and trekkers speaking a half-dozen different languages. Amber and I joined a group of newly arrived trekkers from Bosnia for a dinner of *daal bhat*, a traditional Nepali staple of rice and a spicy lentil stew often made with chicken or goat meat. The rooms were all filled, so we stretched out our sleeping bags on the floor among the porters.

The night was short and we had a long trek in front of us following the terminal moraine of the Khumbu Glacier to Gorak Shep and then EBC. The beautiful triangular peak of Ama Dablam was at our back as the path crossed the top of a ridge covered with memorials to lost climbers and Sherpa. When Amber and I finally reached EBC, we were met by his brother Karna, a mountain guide who had first summited Everest the previous year. He was at EBC waiting for a client from Luxemberg whom he would lead on a summit attempt later in the month.

After dropping my gear in my borrowed tent, I lay down for a nap in the warm late-day sun as the mountains started clouding over. I woke to the clanking of pots and the chatter of an unfamiliar language. Amber and Karna were in the cooking tent with two other Nepali guides and two Indian climbers. I joined the group for a supper of daal bhat. We shared stories and jokes while sipping tea in the flickering light of our headlamps. Darkness came quickly, bringing with it a bone-chilling cold that lasted throughout the night.

For the next two days, I wandered unnoticed around camp. There was no urgency, just the opposite. I witnessed a practiced routine of daily chores familiar to campsites all over the world. I sat for hours marveling as climbers snaked their way around the towers of ice and bottomless crevices of the Kumbu icefall that flows down the slopes of Everest. Mine was a rare opportunity to spend time living among elite high-altitude mountaineers. Most tourist trekkers who visit EBC are content with a short day trek out of Gorak Shep, the last teahouse village on the trail, or they ascend the 18,500-foot (5,643-m) peak Kala Pattar for amazing views of the summit.

Several times each night, I was woken by the rumble of an avalanche. They began with a crack that sounded like a gunshot in the distance, followed by a roll of thunder that swept over the valley like a storm. What a precarious place we had chosen to lay our beds. Well before dawn on my last night at EBC, Karna set out across the icefall to begin preparing his first climbing camp on the Western Cwm, also known as the Valley of Silence. As I listened to the crunching of his footsteps fade into the distance, I contemplated why so many people are prepared to risk so much to challenge themselves against the mountain. It is an old and valid question.

IN 1923, A NEW YORK TIMES REPORTER asked George Mallory the seemingly simple question, "Why do you want to climb Mount Everest?" His often-quoted response has been called the most famous three words in mountaineering, "Because it's there," he quipped. A year later, Everest took his life, along with that of his climbing partner, Andrew "Sandy" Irvine, who disappeared only a few hundred meters from the summit. It wouldn't be until 1953 that New Zealander Edmond Hillary and Sherpa Tenzing Norgay finally reached the summit of Everest and returned safely.

The Everest Highway

As all of the 8,000-meter peaks were conquered, the reason to climb the world's highest mountains shifted from the military-style conquest sponsored by nations, to a more personal test of one's own limits. Italian Reinhold Messner, considered by many to be the greatest climber in history, made the first ascent of Everest without supplemental oxygen in 1978. In 1986, he also became the first person to have summited all fourteen of the world's 8,000-meter peaks. The mountaineering achievements of the '70s and '80s were triumphs of the individual.

The lure of Everest is inexplicable. The little city on a glacier, draped in prayer flags and the national flags of a dozen countries, is just the temporary home to a dream. For climbers, it is a dream to conquer the ultimate peak. For Nepali Sherpa, climbing Everest is a job, a passion, and a dream to earn respect, fame, and money in a desperately poor nation. At almost every teahouse, there is a photograph of a family member who has achieved this dream. It is also the destination of thirty thousand trekkers a year who push themselves harder than they thought possible, struggling against the altitude and elements, for just a passing glimpse of her majesty.

As Amber and I made our way back to Lukla, we made one final stop at Tengboche. Once again, the fog rolled in to shroud my final views of distant mountaintops. In the dimly lit dining room of the lodge, I met Jon, Karna's client from Luxemberg. It was a chance encounter, an unexpected meeting as he made his way toward EBC and his summit attempt. The two of us sat in silence as the stove warmed the still air and raindrops pattered on the steel roof of the building. We were both drawn to Everest and found ourselves together in this particular place, at this particular time. Our pasts and our futures were thousands of miles away. At that moment I realized that although we faced different challenges, the reasons we had come to Everest were our own…ultimately, we came because it's here.

OPPOSITE PAGE: Qaleraliq Glacier, Greenland

Chapter 8
Forces of Change

"The real voyage of discovery consists not in seeking new landscapes but in having new eyes."

—Marcel Proust

Change is a basic law of nature. Environments, animals, cultures, and communities are constantly evolving and adapting to new realities, but change affects individuals and societies in very different ways. From its humble beginnings as a pastime for wealthy aristocrats in the nineteenth century, tourism today has grown into a trillion dollar economic engine and one of the most powerful forces for change in the world. Modern tourism brings together people from different cultures on a scale never before imagined and is central to the lives of millions.

Tourism has many positive impacts, such as raising the standard of living in poor communities, improving infrastructure, preserving historical sites, and raising awareness of environmental issues, but change in fragile places needs to be both managed and mutually beneficial. As tourists and photographers, our choices and actions can, and do, have a direct effect on the people and places we visit. Nowhere is the tourist impact more visible and sensitive than in the world's most remote places.

Sometimes, the desire to attract tourists, and the money they bring with them, can leave in its wake broken environments and conflicted indigenous communities. In both cases, tourism might be the solution or create a bigger problem. Tourist travel can be a powerful and positive force for change, but only when we tread lightly through the world that beckons so intensely. Finding the balance between using natural resources to attract tourists and preserving them is a challenging proposition.

The Enchanted Isles

The towering peak of La Cumbre was hidden behind a vaporous cloak of dense fog, intensifying the mysterious stillness as our "panga" shuttled us toward an unearthly landscape. We carefully made our way across the slick, hardened lava, taking our first tentative steps along the rugged coastline of Fernandina. In the cracks and shadows where the volcano meets the sea, some of the strangest creatures imaginable took notice of our presence. We had entered a prehistoric world where amphibious dragons lair and exotic life clings to the sharp edge of an unforgiving home.

As the nighttime chill began to yield to the equatorial sun, Fernandina awakened, and the world's only sea-lizards revealed themselves through subtle movements and periodic spurts to clear salt from their nostrils. The rocks were spitting. Hundreds of spiny marine iguana draped the barren earth as we followed a marked trail over fields of swirling pahoehoe lava, punctuated by the occasional pioneering lava cactus.

Fernandina is the youngest and most inhospitable of all the Galápagos Islands. It is an active volcanic wasteland that grows at the very heart of a geothermal hot spot, straddling a complex series of tectonic plates and underwater ridges. Over millions of years, primordial forces have spewed a superheated magma, uplifting the Galápagos platform and exposing the visible summits of undersea volcanoes.

From the oldest in the east to the youngest in the west, the thirteen major islands and over 100 smaller islets and rocks of the archipelago are scattered over 200 miles (320 km) and moving southeast with the shifting oceanic plates at a rate of four centimeters a year. This slow and sometimes violent journey along a geologic conveyor belt is evidence of a living planet. The Galápagos Islands are still changing, still evolving, and still adapting to unpredictable forces now witnessed and directly influenced by a growing number of curious travelers from around the world.

The small group of nature lovers I joined onboard the twenty-passenger expedition yacht called Flamingo 1 were just beginning to bond as we continued our walk over the cracked and eroded lava, overwhelmed by the desolate beauty of Fernandina. As we neared the north shore of Punta Espinosa, I stopped to photograph young sea lions frolicking in a small inlet and flightless cormorant warming their wings on the rocky shore. For a few brief moments, I was separated from the constant digital news feeds, cell phones, and computer networks of the modern era and left with a sense of amazement at the timeless complexity of the natural world around me.

As the late morning sun broke through the haze, I could finally see Isabela, Fernandina's giant island neighbor to the east, and the looming summit of La Cumbre. Everywhere, it seemed, the once motionless iguana were repositioning themselves for maximum exposure to the warming rays of the rising sun or scurrying into the water for a breakfast of algae. The increasingly intense light exaggerated the already brilliant colors of sally lightfoot crab, framed against a pallet of black, as they ducked into small fissures and holes to avoid the advancing parade of tourists.

We slowly circled back to the small rubber raft that would become our familiar shuttle to and from Flamingo 1. Our afternoon was spent snorkeling off the coast of Isabela with sea lions, turtles, and Galápagos penguin in the protected Tagus Cove. In a routine that would be repeated throughout the voyage, we gathered for dinner, shared stories and pictures, and were under way as the sun began to set. We traveled the open ocean in darkness and at first light found ourselves on the doorstep of a new and fascinating island world.

IN FEBRUARY OF 1535, JUST THREE years after the conquest of Peru by Francisco Pizzaro, the Spanish bishop of Panama, Fray

Tomás de Berlanga, was becalmed in the equatorial doldrums en route to Lima. His ship was seized by the cold ocean stream of the South Equatorial Current and drifted 620 miles (1,000 km) west of the South American coast into the deep uncharted Pacific. On March 10th, he unintentionally discovered the Galápagos.

The bishop's accounts of a brutal place with no fresh water and strange animals are the first known records of human beings setting foot on the islands. Early visitors referred to them as "Las Encantadas," the Bewitched Islands, because phantom silhouettes seemed to appear and disappear unexplainably on the ocean horizon and volcanic peaks vanished as if by magic in the distant fog.

Others still called them "hell on Earth," a place so hostile to human life that the best recourse was to plunder and leave. It was described as a treacherous place of legend, where unknown forces conspired to create giant tortoises, hideous serpents, and flightless birds. It was a lost world, without man, and seemingly inconsistent with a divine plan or intelligent design. For hundreds of years, seafarers used the Galápagos as a hideout, refuge, or base of operations, often stopping only long enough to resupply on tortoise meat and "foolishly tame wildlife," as described by Tomás.

By the time a young 26-year-old Charles Darwin visited the Galápagos in 1835, there had been three centuries of human interaction with the islands. The bizarre wildlife now shared their geologic oasis with pirates, whalers, fur sealers, convicts, and castaways, but the islands had never been successfully settled. Although several nonendemic species like goats and rats had been introduced to the Islands, Darwin found a nearly intact ecosystem largely unaffected by the hand of man. Not only was there an abundance of unique species, but identifiable variation from island to island. He and others later theorized that the very diversity of species and subspecies illustrated how populations adapted to ecological niches.

Darwin's observations changed much more than the prevailing view of a distant and mysterious archipelago. They revealed a secret so seemingly simple yet so controversial that it has changed our understanding of the world in which we live. His revolutionary thesis, *On the Origin of Species by Means of Natural Selection,* suggests that natural selection combined with inherent genetic variation is the mechanism that allows species under stress and in isolation to change over time, overcoming the challenges of their local environment.

Generation after generation, individuals better suited to live in the hostile environments of the Galápagos passed along traits that would give their decedents a competitive advantage—an edge toward long-term survival. The dramatic shifts and cycles of the ocean currents that converge on the archipelago both feed the incredible diversity of life and lead to drastic population crashes and rebounds that clearly favor the fittest. But the islands are a fragile jewel.

ON MOST ISLANDS OF THE GALÁPAGOS, visitors, prohibited from any sort of personal inland exploration, follow a narrow band of marked trails where they discover the best-known creatures of the coast. On the weatherworn and lightly visited southernmost Island of Española, the tourist trail leads past blue-footed boobies, fledgling waved albatross, and the bleached bones of earlier generations to a stunning vista of soaring seabirds and ragged coastline. Almost the entire world population of waved albatross live and breed on Española. They follow the shifting currents of the Humboldt and spend nearly half the year at sea feeding on squid. They return to Española in April to mate and raise their young. By December, they again take to the wing and follow the Humboldt Current to their feeding grounds off the coasts of Peru and Chile.

Every visitor is touched in unexpected ways by the mysterious wonders and natural surprises that have been island gifts to the observant for centuries. Very few of us have ever had any real interaction with wildlife in their natural environments. Somewhere along the way, we became civilized and lost our familiarity with the forces of nature just outside the protective walls of our society. We look at animals in simulated environments and view spectacular landscapes from guardrails at posted overlooks or the balcony of an all-inclusive resort. We are tourists of nature.

In the Galápagos, I encountered animals with no visible fear or anxiety inspired by my close encounter, a genetic innocence that has evolved in the absence of man. I experienced a raw and intimate connection to a place where the cycles of life and death are not hidden by walls of civilization, but experienced, naked and authentic, just meters and moments away. I watched as a suckling newborn sea lion pup drifted in and out of a peaceful sleep as the click of my camera introduced a modern sound to an ancient world.

Hour after hour, day after day, I was captivated by the inquisitive stare of a young waved albatross and the paternal dominance exhibited by a male sea lion patrolling his small section of sandy beach on an island speck in a massive ocean. A short distance away the broken wing of a struggling seabird foretold a certain death, while an enthusiastic booby couple began their courtship with an amusing display of affection. I cherished the fleeting moments of simple observation, knowing that species have come and gone, adapted and died in a constant chain of interconnected events for millions of years without human witness.

AS OUR JOURNEY ABOARD Flamingo 1 neared its eventual end, we were surprised to be joined by Santiago Dunn, the owner of Ecoventura. He was in the islands for the maiden voyage of his new solar-powered sister ship, *Eric*, the first of its kind in the Galápagos. After a wonderful dinner, we all gathered in the main sitting area adjacent to the dining room and once again shared photographs and experiences. We had gotten to know each other quite well, so the conversation was easy and enthusiastic. We welcomed Santiago's personal stories and watched a stunning underwater video shot off the coast of neighboring Wolf Island by Alexis, one of our expert guides and a master diver.

As the night grew longer, our conversation shifted to a more somber discussion about the future of the Galápagos. It was impossible not to notice the large congregation of cruise liners, tankers, and tourists at the bustling port of Puerto Ayora on Santa Cruz. Most of us were unaware of the forces of change that are now influencing the delicate balance of life in the archipelago. There is growing concern among scientists and conservationists that uncontrolled tourism, expanding resident populations, pollution, and over-fishing may seriously threaten the islands.

The exploitation that began hundreds of years ago by pirates and whalers continues today with the brutal and senseless slaughter of nearly a million sharks every year that are "finned" alive and dumped back into the water to bleed an agonizing death. In the Galápagos Marine Reserve, tens of thousands of fins have been seized in a single shipment and endangered sea lions are often used as bait, solely to feed the appetite for shark fin soup, or what is more commonly known as "fish wing" soup in some parts of Asia.

But illegal shark poaching isn't the only emerging threat to the once isolated ecosystem. Annual tourism has grown from 40,000 visitors to over 140,000 in just the past fifteen years. This worldwide interest has also swelled the resident population to over 30,000, accompanied by new predator populations of dogs and cats. New and potentially fatal diseases have also arrived with humans and their pets. There is a now-constant flow of food, energy, and resources to support this permanent colonization.

In one of the greatest ironies of human history, the place that inspired centuries of investigation, research, and reflection into the very nature of our existence, may ultimately be destroyed by our very presence. The Galápagos is a unique and special world protected for millennia by its isolation. It is unlike any other place on earth. But now the islands are no longer feared, no longer a secret to a modern world with jet aircraft and the wealth to travel. Sometimes by intent, more often through ignorance, we are destroyers of worlds.

Conservation, education, and visitation are all essential components in the struggle to control and manage one of the great living museums on earth. While turning back the clock to a time before our intrusion into this prehistoric world is not an option, the Galápagos National Park Service and Charles Darwin Foundation, in conjunction with the United Nations and dozens of NGOs, are aggressively initiating programs to seek answers to difficult problems and lessen the impact of essential tourism. As tourists of nature in a world with very few remaining secrets, we are now forced to question our own responsibility as enlightened stewards of the world over which we hold dominion.

Naked *by* Choice

We marched for hours through the high grass and endless scrub of the central Kalahari. The "Old Man," as he is known in the village, stopped only briefly to examine a small dent in the sandy soil or inspect the trace of a passing animal. He moved gracefully over the inhospitable land with a confidence that comes from centuries of accumulated knowledge. We followed at a distance as he scanned the horizon, silently tracking something in the immeasurable distance. "Kudo," announced our young, English-speaking Ju/'hoan-San guide, pointing to a wooded area silhouetted against the strong glare of the morning sun.

They are known around the world as Bushmen, but this derogatory term referring to the African hunter-gatherers of myth and legend

has recently lost much of its negative connotation. The San Bushmen are one of the oldest populations on earth and one of the most thoroughly studied groups of indigenous people in the history of anthropology. Once called "living fossils" by nineteenth-century western scholars and advertised as the last link to our ancient hunter-gather existence, the San have been a fascination and curiosity ever since the first stories and pictures of small, nearly naked Africans circulated the world a century ago.

Today, there are approximately 85,000 to 100,000 San living in six southern African countries, where they have been largely marginalized from the modern world. Ju/'hoan is a branch of the click language, Khoisan, which is spoken in northeast Namibia and the northwest region of Botswana (/' refers to a click sound in Ju/'hoan language). The Ju/'hoan of the Nyae Nyae region, as they prefer to be called, are the second largest group of San Bushmen in Namibia and continue to reside on a small portion of their ancestral lands near the Botswana border.

It didn't take long for our cool morning walk to turn into a scorching trek across the sun–beaten savanna. Barefoot and standing no more than five feet tall, the Old Man was remarkably fit. His hair was mostly gray and his leathery skin exhibited scratches and scars acquired through years of battle with the desert. As we walked, he identified several of the nearly one hundred species of edible plants, nuts, fruits, and tubers that were the staple foods of his ancestors.

DRESSED IN AN ANIMAL-SKIN LOINCLOTH, carrying a bow and quiver of arrows, the Old Man was, in fact, leading our small group on what the tourist program described as a "Hunting Trip." Presented in the menu of options as a full day of walking in the wild trying to catch "warthog, kudu, springhare, porcupine or whatever might be so careless to cross our way," it was one of eight experiences available to visitors at the Living Hunter's Museum of the Ju/'hoan San in the Nyae Nyae Conservancy.

As we stopped for a short break from the midday sun and warm Kalahari wind, it was becoming apparent that our bush experience would be more about tracking than actually hunting. "There are not as many animals anymore," noted our young guide. Resting under a large baobab tree, this realization brought an end to the hunt and gave us a chance to ask the Old Man about his life in the Kalahari and what modern San refer to as the "Old Way."

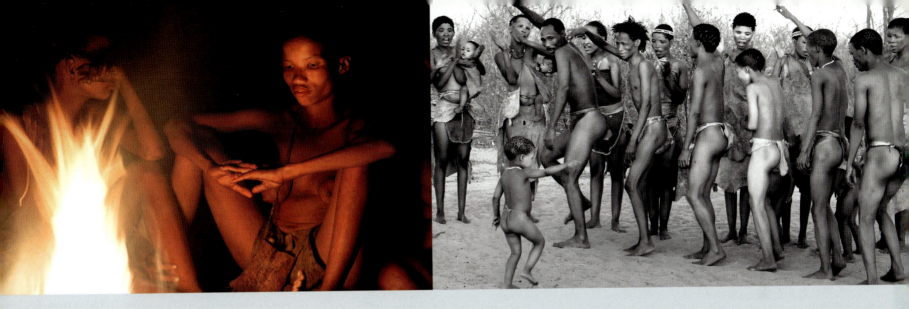

The Ju/'hoansi who live in the Nyae Nyae Conservancy are the only San officially allowed to hunt in their traditional way on their ancestral lands, but it has been over a half century since bands roamed freely living off the land throughout the Namibian Kalahari. While their ancestors had been traveling through the veld hunting and gathering food for tens of thousands of years, prior to Namibian independence from South African rule in 1990, the San had few rights to land, resources, or wildlife.

As the young nation grew out of the ashes of nearly seventy years of oppression under apartheid, the Namibian government demonstrated a strong commitment to further the rights of historically disadvantaged indigenous people. They initiated programs to deliver educational support, water development, food, and pensions to the elderly.

After years of conversation and debate, legislation for a new natural resource management structure known as a conservancy was passed in 1996. It allowed for local communities to form conservancies to both manage and benefit from wildlife and tourism on multi-use communal land. In June of 1998, the Nyae Nyae region became the first conservancy in Namibia, and for the first time a small group of former hunter-gatherers had the right to make decisions about the use of their ancestral lands.

OUR SMALL GROUP SAT UNDER THE BAOBAB TREE for quite a while talking with the Old Man through our translator guide. It was a forward-thinking San named !Amace who initiated The Living Hunter's Museum in 2010 after studying the success of Namibia's first living museum, which had opened a few years prior. With the help of the German-Namibian organization, Living Culture Foundation Namibia, the community at //Xa/oba entered the tourism industry. "We were very poor," !Amace later told me. "Now almost everyone in the village is a part of the museum."

In addition to the hunting experience, programs at the museum include learning to light a fire, making ropes and snares, shooting with a bow and arrow, searching for bush food, traditional singing and dancing, and storytelling around a campfire. Each experience has an associated price. In addition to hunting, our group also selected traditional dancing and storytelling. After a short rest back at our campsite, we made our way through the bush toward the distant sound of song. Nearly half the village was

waiting in their traditional dress (or more accurately, mostly undressed) at the replica village of their ancestors. I mounted my camera on a tripod as the sun began to set.

Following a short introduction by !Amace, several generations of Ju/'hoansi sang and danced in the soft sand. The Old Man and the village healer sat quietly by a small campfire. Naked children ran, jumped, and wrestled at their parent's feet. Several women nursed infants as they clapped to the desultory ballet. The scene had all the romantic and exotic flavor of a first contact with an ancient lost tribe. It was an intoxicating display.

While the large group danced and enjoyed themselves as if our cameras weren't there, this was clearly a performance inspired by our tourist visit. I was happily clicking away, taking pictures of "small, nearly naked Africans" just like those that inspired foolishly considered comments like "living fossils" so many years ago. I also understood that without proper context my images could easily perpetuate the myth that the descendants of some of the earliest humans to inhabit Southern Africa were still living idyllic, isolated lives untouched by history.

On the surface, images of Ju/'hoansi dressed in their traditional costumes might appear to perpetuate the antiquated and insensitive narrative of the uncivilized African savage suspended in a perpetual state of nakedness, but the story isn't quite that simple. The Ju/'hoan "actors" performing in pseudo tourist events are only one generation removed from the lifestyle they depict. Their authenticity is raw and comes from a renewed pride in their culture of antiquity. They are naked by choice. The have chosen to perform for tourists and in so doing are changing the perception of their people from a primitive curiosity to the protectors of ancient wisdom. The young children I photographed had no understanding that they were a part of a tourist performance; they were simply dancing with their brothers and sisters like their tribe had for generations.

"Sadly," "unfortunately," and "regrettably" are all terms recently used in modern media to refer to the fact that the Bushmen of the Kalahari can no longer live the life of hunter-gatherers, implying that the San of today would be content with the ways of the past. But while we were sitting under the baobab tree, I asked the Old Man what it was like to live the Old Way. He answered without hesitation, "Living in the bush is hard. The children were almost always hungry. Life is better now," he added with a nod.

FOR THE JU/'HOAN ELDERS in the village of //Xa/oba, the Living Hunter's Museum is a positive and authentic recreation of their old way of life. They say that their old ways give meaning to their lives and connect them through generations. The museum is a workplace and entrepreneurial business that they own and control. The profits are shared among the community. !Amace says the tourist performances and storytelling are also "a way for us to pass on our culture without it being lost forever." San children from all over the region come with their schoolmates to learn about their long and fascinating past. The oral history and traditions of the San are being recorded by elders in their native tongue and written down for future generations. Even the word *Bushmen* is being ennobled by the Ju/'hoansi themselves to refer to their great environmental knowledge and bush skills.

It is easy to embrace the romantic notion that indigenous cultures should be preserved and tribal people, even those on the edge of existence, should be allowed to live in peace like their ancestors have for centuries. But for communities that live hard lives in inhospitable places, more abundant food, clean drinking water, better medicines, less infant mortality, education, and a longer life expectancy should not be interpreted as unfortunate effects of modernity on a romanticized indigenous culture.

All over the world, tribal communities are facing a similar balancing act of trying to preserve their ancient cultural past while educating their children to compete in a modern, digital world, wearing trousers and skirts instead of loincloths. Increasingly, indigenous tribes are taking control of their tourist product and the image of their culture that is presented for tourist consumption. Although they remain very poor by most international measures, the conservancy has supplied jobs and income for many and has allowed the Ju/'hoansi living in the Nyae Nyae to have a choice about their future and a voice in how their destiny unfolds.

OPPOSITE PAGE LEFT TO RIGHT: Kolkata, India; Beijing, China; Xinjiang, China; Namibia
BELOW: Ghandruk, Nepal

Final Word

"Education is the most powerful weapon which you can use to change the world."

—Nelson Mandela

Through Innocent Eyes

It was late morning when my trekking group left the village of Ghandruk in the Middle Hills of Nepal. Our route out of town just happened to cross in front of a small brick house with a crude stone porch. A young girl was waving enthusiastically as we approached. She hopped down the stairs and started running toward us, stopping abruptly in front of me at what must have felt like a safe distance. For a few seconds, the two of us just looked at each other, neither exactly sure what to do next. It was a chance encounter between two very different people who had lived very different lives. The only thing we had in common was a curiosity about the other.

After the first awkward moments passed, I pointed to the camera I was holding. She smiled and offered a gentle nod of permission. As I raised the camera to my eye, she steepled her hands in front of her face and said quietly, "Namaste." As soon as I lowered my camera, she turned and scampered back into her house, peeking from the doorway as I continued down the trail. For one brief moment in time, our paths had crossed and our lives had intersected.

Our lives are almost continuously shaped and affected by unexpected and unplanned experiences and chance encounters. Some touch us only lightly, while others can change the trajectory of our lives. As travelers we can choose certain types of experiences, but we have no control over the element of chance. The simple gift of a portrait from a beautiful girl in Brazil and a spontaneous smile of a frightened little boy in Kenya are special moments from my first travel experiences that altered the course of my career.

These two seemingly insignificant encounters with children living under totally different circumstances on opposite ends of the world were the beginning of a chain of events that inspired me to travel and search for something a bit more "real" in my life than the make-believe world of advertising. My journey to Kenya, which started as a personal challenge to expand my knowledge of the world and become a better photographer, ended with an understanding that for many children in the developing world, the "real" I was looking for is often harsh and unforgiving. We enter their world for only a brief moment and then we go home, taking with us our pictures and memories but often leaving nothing behind.

As a photographer and travel writer, I have been able to see and share the reality of life on earth from a comfortable distance—the distance that comes from placing a camera between me

The Photographing Tourist **203**

and the poverty I was witnessing and the distance that comes from the knowledge that I would soon be going back to my comfortable home. It is inherent in the tourist experience that it is only temporary, but my desire to "remain a detached and objective witness," as I suggested in the introduction, ended the very first day I got down on my knees and played with the beautiful children in a remote Samburu village.

It is impossible to travel into remote corners of the developing world and not be touched by the innocent eyes of a young child. Every tourist I have led into a poor and underserved community has asked, "What can we do to help?" Every village elder and community leader I have asked that question returns with the same answer: "Help educate the children." Often, governments in the developing world don't have the resources to reach into these remote communities, and with so many disasters and crises around the globe, it is not surprising that less than 2 percent of the world's humanitarian aid goes to the education sector. Education is also a long-term commitment. It can take a decade or more before a young child who goes to school for the first time will grow up to contribute to his or her community.

UNESCO (United Nations Educational, Scientific, and Cultural Organization) reports that

OPPOSITE PAGE LEFT TO RIGHT, TOP TO BOTTOM: Xinjiang, China; Costa Rica; Dominica; Dominica; Myanmar; Xinjiang, China; Guatemala; Tibet; Namibia

two billion children, 85 percent of the world's total, live in the developing world. Their futures and the futures of their children depend on whether or not they go to school and how much they learn. In 2000, the World Education Forum in Dakar committed 164 nations to achieving free universal basic education by 2015. While a tremendous amount has been done, there is still a lot to do. One hundred million children of primary school age are not in school, and nearly half of the world's out-of-school children live in sub-Saharan Africa. Children in many of the world's poorest countries can spend several years in school without learning to read a word, and of the 796 million illiterate people in the world today, over two-thirds of them are women.

It is easy to forget that behind every statistic there are young people who don't have a chance to fulfill their potential. But education is much more than simply having the opportunity to attend school; for many of the world's poorest children, it is the only chance they have to acquire the basic skills needed to find off-farm work, earn a living, and forever break the cycle of poverty. Unfortunately, the kids who would benefit the most from an education often don't have access to schools, or teachers, or books. This is even more complicated within tribal communities that are struggling to retain some of their ancient cultural past while attempting to prepare their children to compete in the twenty-first century.

Throughout my travels, I have made an effort to photograph the young kids I was encountering. Increasingly, the stories I was most interested in telling were about the children I was meeting along the edges of my adventures; the marginalized children who were watching from a distance as I navigated through a packaged tour of their world…and leaving nothing behind. While stories and images can enlighten, inform, inspire, and educate, they rarely change the reality of life of those depicted. For me, that wasn't enough. I determined that I could do more than show my pictures or tell a story; I could actually help change the course of a young life.

In 2013, I launched Innocent Eyes Project, Inc. It is a US-based nonprofit charity to support grassroots child education programs in developing countries, where small amounts of money can make a real difference in the lives of children. With this project, I have joined the global initiative to help children of the world receive a quality education. I am no longer just a storyteller, I am a part of the story. It is a story about the hopes and dreams of children and families. It is also a story about the gift we share as travelers to experience the world and our desire to give back to the people and places that have touched our lives.

While still a young organization, Innocent Eyes Project was already making a difference in the lives of children by funding the construction of the first schoolhouse in Lugala, Uganda; supporting the education of children in Kenya, Tanzania, and Guatemala; and funding a school lunch program for the beautiful kids of Camoapa, Nicaragua.

Clearly, our efforts can't begin to confront the enormous global child education issues requiring billions of dollars and governmental resources, but our charity isn't about rescuing a continent or a country, it is about giving one child at a time a chance at a better life by getting an education, and sometimes that education can only be acquired through the generosity of others. Like the small ripple that spirals outward when a pebble is tossed into the water, educating one child in a remote corner of the world can truly touch the lives of thousands.

To learn more about Innocent Eyes Project or to become involved in helping to educate children who live along the edges of your adventures, visit:

OPPOSITE PAGE: Moshi, Tanzania

Index

A

abandoned places, 39, 48, 113, 121
acacia trees, 15, 146
action shots, 163, 165
action/adventure tourism, 161–182
    Greenland, 152–159
    Himalayas, 174–181
adrenaline rush, 9, 54, 86, 90, 149, 153
Africa, *xiii*
    child education issues, 205
    Kalahari bushmen, 194–201
    Kikuyu, *xi*, 14
    Namibia, 6, 24, 133, 202
    safari, 15, 17–18, 144–151
    See also Kenya; Tanzania
Agra, India, *x*, 56
agriculture, subsistence, 47–48
Alaska, 109, 170–171
alms and offerings, 79–80, 85, 90, 103, 178
altitude, extreme, 162, 167, 169
anchors in landscape photography, 134
angle of view, 3, 22
    distinguished from point of view, 26
    horizons, 166
animals and wildlife, 15, 27–29, 139–141
    animal rights, 28
    in the Galápagos, 138, 184–193
    as part of destination narrative, 141
    safari, 15, 17–18, 144–151
Annapurna range, 44
anxiety regarding photography, *xi*, *xiii*
aperture, 111, 136
architecture, sacred, 77–78, 127
arctic conditions, 152–159, 182
artificial light, 78
    flash photography, 79, 81
Athens, Greece, 106
authenticity, *xi*, *xiii*, 22–23, 59, 63, 119, 199
auto focus, 114
Ayutthaya, Thailand, 111

B

background, as element of design, 57
backlight, 7, 136
backup equipment, 162
Bagan, Myanmar, *xii*, 58, 80, 84–85
Bahia, Brazil, 54
balance, as principle of design, 60
Basilica of Saint Mark's, 129
bathers, 70, 79, 90
battery/electricity requirements, 162, 167, 169
beggars, hawkers, and scammers, *xiii*, 23–24, 65–66, 69, 73, 89, 93, 97
behind-the-scenes photographs, 61, 110
Beijing, *xi*, 5, 22, 110–111, 114, 119, 202
"being in the zone," 9
Belize, 133
Bewitched Islands, 188
Birethanti, Nepal, 20
blind shots, 114
Block, Lewis, quote, 131
boredom, 9
Brahma Temple, 69
Brazil, 54
breaking the ice, 4
Brim, William, 24
Buddhism and Buddhist traditions, 80, 83, 85, 93, 101, 103, 178
bullseye effect, 5
"burning ghat," 94

C

Calcutta (Kolkata), 59–60, 64–65, 202
camels, 28, 66–74
Cancun, Mexico, 3, 8
Cartier-Bresson, Henri, quote, 53
catch-light, 81
ceremonial objects, 83, 178
change in fragile places, impact of tourism, 183–205
charity supporting education programs in developing countries, 205
Chesterton, Gilbert K., 2
Chiang Mai, Thailand, 23, 79
Chiang Rai, Thailand, 29, 61
Chichen Itza, Mexico, *viii*, 116
Chichicastenango, Guatemala, 22
children
    education issues in poor countries, 204–205
    photographing, 11, 23–24, 30–31, 49, 54, 65
China, 118–119
    Beijing, *xi*, 5, 22, 110–111, 114, 119, 202
    Cultural Revolution, 101
    Great Wall, 119
    Hotan, 5, 40
    Kashgar, 6, 35–36, 58
    Maoist movement, 48
    Silk Road, 34–43
    Tibet, *viii*, 26, 58, 81, 98–105
    Xinjiang, 39, 42, 202, 204
Chomolungma, 177
churches. *See* sacred and religious sites
cigar manufacturing, 54
"civilized" cultures, 27
clichéd photographs, 108
climate change, 154–159
clothing, traditional, 23, 25, 61, 79–80, 83, 87
clouds in landscape photography, 132
cold, extreme conditions, 162, 167, 169
color, as element of design, 57
color-compensating filters, 78, 138, 166
Colosseum, 112
composition, 57
    bullseye effect, 5
    defined, 3
    landscape photography, 134
    line, 135
    rule of thirds, 5
condensation, 169
content of photographs, 4, 163
    vs. presentation, 6
contextual aides, 22, 58, 113, 117, 199
Costa Rica, 166
cremation ceremony, 90, 94, 97
crocodile, 149
cruise vacations, 109–110, 127, 171, 190
cultural etiquette and sensitivity, 11, 21, 23, 27, 76, 79
Cultural Revolution of China, 101
curves, as design element, 114
Cuzco, Perú, *xii*, 59

D

danger, sense of, 161
Darwin, Charles, 188
Dead Sea, 134
decorative photography, 6
definitions
    adventure, 161
    itinerary, 2
    tourist, 1
depth of field, 111, 136
deserts
    desert tribes, 27–28
    Namib Desert, 6, 133
    Negev Desert, 27, 52, 132, 135
    Taklamakan Desert, 39–40, 169
design elements, 57
design principles, 60
detachment, *xiii*, 4
details and contextual aides, 113, 117
diffusers, 81
digital photography, 4
filtered effects, 78, 138, 166
high-dynamic-range (HDR) imaging, 138
distance, maintaining, 53
diving and snorkeling, 163, 165–167
Dominica, *xii*, 165
Drepung, 100–101
dress, traditional, 23, 25, 61, 79–80, 83, 87
dust and sand damage, 169

E

Eastman, George, 2
editorial photography, 110
education needs in poor countries, 204–205
Eid al-Adha, 35–36
electricity and battery requirements, 162, 167, 169
elements of design, 57
elephants, 15, 27–28
Emerson, Ralph Waldo, quote, 107
emotional responses, 56
empathy and shared humanity, *ix*, 21, 32, 59, 63, 83, 203–205
emphasis, as principle of design, 60
"Las Encantadas," 188
environmental context, 58–59
environmental portraits
    animals, 141
    explained, 58
Ephesus, Turkey, 108
equipment protection in adventure tourism, 162
ethnic communities. *See* tribal/ethnic communities
Everest, 48, 174–181
Everest Base Camp (EBC), 174, 177–178
everyday life, 55, 59, 61
exploitation, 23, 42, 190
exposure, 136
    active/adventure photography, 166

The Photographing Tourist **207**

landscape photography, 134, 139
  overexposure, 139
  sidelight and backlight, 7
  See also light
extreme conditions, 162, 167, 169
  arctic conditions, 152–159
  Mount Everest, 48, 174–181
  See also deserts
eye contact, 3, 63, 66, 141
eye-level view, 22

F

faces and facial expressions, 61, 63, 137
fees/payments for photographing, *xi*, 23–24, 58, 61, 63, 66, 69, 80
fill flash, 81
filters
  color-compensating filters, 78, 138, 166
  UV filters, 169
fishbowl effect, 22, 27
fjords, 153
flash photography, 79, 81
"flat" light, 7
focal length, 3
focus, controlling, 111
fog and mist, landscape photography, 134, 139
fogging on lenses, 169
foreground, as element of design, 57
form, as element of design, 57
framing, 3, 113
f-stop, 111
funeral ceremony, 90, 94, 97

G

Galápagos, 138, 184–193
game safari, 15, 17–18, 144–151
Ganges River, 90, 93–94, 97
gathering places, 53–74
gaze/eye contact, 3, 63, 66, 141
Gernsheim, Helmut, quote, 21
Ghandruk, Nepal, 203
glaciers, 152–159, 182
  arctic conditions, 152–159, 182
  chapter 6 nature's spectacle, 131–160
global child education issues, 204–205
gnu (wildebeest), 144–146, 149–150
"The Goddess Mother of the World," 177

golden hour, landscape photography, 136–137
gondolas, 129
Gongkar Monastery, 81
"good" *vs.* "bad" light, 9
governments in developing countries, resources of, 204
graduated neutral density filter, 138
Grand Canal, 125–126
Great Wall of China, 119
Greece, 106
Greenland, 152–159
guided or escorted tours, 1
Gurkha soldiers, 49
gypsies, gods, and dromedaries, 66–74

H

Hagia Sofia, Turkey, 77
The Hall of Prayer for Good Harvests, China, 108
hawkers, beggars, and scammers, *xiii*, 23–24, 65–66, 69, 73, 89, 93, 97
heat, extreme conditions, 162, 167, 169
high-dynamic-range (HDR) imaging, 138
highlights and shadows, 3, 78, 132–133, 136, 138
Himalayas, 48, 174–181
Hindu traditions and Hinduism, 69–70, 88–97
history of photography, 2, 4
holy places. *See* sacred and religious sites
Hopkins, Belize, 133
horizon line, 166
horizontal line, 114
Hotan, China, 5, 40
houses of worship. *See* sacred and religious sites
human connection/empathy, *ix*, 21, 32, 59, 63, 83, 203–205
humor and irony, 56
hunter-gatherers, 194–201

I

ice flows and formations, 152–159
Iceland, 139, 142, 164, 167
iconic places, 107, 109–110
Id Kah Mosque, 35–36, 77
immersiveness, 2, 6

impact of tourism, 183–205
Inca trail. *See* Perú
India, *xii*, 64–74, 88–97
  Hindu traditions and Hinduism, 69–70, 88–97
  Kolkata, 59–60, 64–65, 202
  social system, 97
indigenous tourism, 27
  See also tribal/ethnic communities
Inle Lake, Myanmar, 137–138, 140
Innocent Eyes Project, 205
instinct and reaction, *xiii*
Isla Chira, Costa Rica, 5
Islam, 35–36, 39
Israel
  Jerusalem, *ix*, 55, 86–87
  Negev Desert, 27, 52, 132, 135
Italy
  Pompeii, 117
  Venice, 122–129
itineraries, challenges of fixed plans, 108

J

Jerusalem, *ix*, 55, 86–87
the Jokhang, 101, 103
Ju/'hoansi, 194–201
Juneau, Alaska, 109

K

Kalaw, Myanmar, 28
Karakoram Highway, 39
Karen tribe, 30–32
Kartik Purnima, 70
Kashgar, 6, 35–36, 58
Kathmandu, 48
kayaking and rafting, 163, 165
Kayan tribe, 31–32
Kentucky, 164, 168
Kenya, *xi*, *xiii*, 10–20, 145, 149
  Lake Nakuru, 146
  safari, 15, 17–18, 144–151
  Samburu, 11, 140, 142, 146
Khao Lak, Thailand, *x*
Khumbu Region, Nepal, 82
Kikuyu, *xi*, 14
Kodak, 4
Kolkata, India, 59–60, 64–65, 202
Kublai Khan, 39, 119

L

Lake Nakuru, 146
landmarks and famous places, 107–130
landscape photography, 131–160
"Las Encantadas," 188
Lhasa, Tibet, *viii*, 58, 100, 103–104
Library of Celsus, Turkey, 108
lifestyles of local cultures, 21–52
light, 3, 6–9, 78–79, 117
  active/adventure tourism, 165–166
  artificial, 57
  flash photography, 79, 81
  landscape photography, 132–133, 136–137
  sidelight and backlight, 7
  See also exposure
Limuru, *xi*
line, as element of design, 57, 135
literacy, global child education issues, 204–205
local lifestyles, 21–52
long lenses, 78
"long-neck Karen," 30–32
Lord Shiva, 88–97
Louvre Museum, 115

M

Maasai Mara National Reserve, 141, 144–151
Maasai tribe, 12–20
Machu Picchu, 109, 121
Maho Beach, Saint Martin, *xiv*, 57
Mallory, Gregory, 178–179
manhood, rite of passage, 18
manipulation of images. *See* digital photography
Maoist movement, 48
Marco Polo, 39
markets and bazaars, 36, 40, 55, 103
matrix metering, 136
meditation, 79, 104
memory and storage issues, 162
metering systems, 136
middle ground, as element of design, 57
mid-tones, 136
mist and fog, landscape photography, 134, 139

modernity, effects of, 119, 194–201
monks and monasteries, 80, 83, 100–101, 103–104, 178
mood of photograph, 63
mosques, 35–36, 77
Mother Teresa, 64–65
Mount Cook, New Zealand, 130
Mount Everest, 48, 174–181
Mount Kilimanjaro, Tanzania, 162
mountain sickness, 178
mountain travel
  Himalayas, 174–181
  Nepal, 40–52
movement, as principle of design, 60
multiple exposures, 138
"must-have" photographs, 54
Myanmar, 31–32, 84–85
  Bagan, *xii*, 58, 80, 84–85
  Inle Lake, 137–138, 140
  Kalaw, 28
  Sulamani Temple, 74

N

Namche, 174
Namibia, 6, 24, 133, 202
narrative photographs, 110, 117
Narsaq, Greenland, *ix*
national destination branding, 27
natural light, 117
natural resources, use to attract tourism, 183
nature. *See* landscape photography
navigating an image, 111
neck rings, 30–32
negative space
  as element of design, 57
  landscape photography, 139
Negev Desert, Israel, 27, 52, 132, 135
Nepal, 40–52, 174–181, 203
New Zealand, 135, 166
nomadic groups, 66–74
nonprofit charity to support child education programs, 205
Notre-Dame Cathedral, 78

O

objective observer point of view, 26
overexposure, 139

P

Palazzo Ducale, 127
Pamir Mountains, 39
Paris, 26
    Louvre, 115
    Notre-Dame Cathedral, 78
Parthenon, 106
participant point of view, 26
payments for photographing, *xi*, 23–24, 58, 61, 63, 66, 69, 80
peer-to-peer interactions, 63
permission to photograph, 54, 65, 203
perspective, 117, 163
    angle of view, 22
Perú, 120–121, 168
    Cuzco, *xii*, 59
    Machu Picchu, 109, 121
    Patallaqta, 62
Phang Nga, Thailand, *x*
Phuket, Thailand, 29, 81
physical condition of photographer, 162
Piazza San Marco, 126–127
pilgrims and pilgrimages, 70, 75, 86–87, 97, 100, 103
point of view, 26
Pompeii, Italy, 117
porters, 44, 177–178
ports of call, 109
positive space, as element of design, 57
Potala Palace, 98, 100, 104
potters, 65
poverty, *xiii*, 204–205
prayer, 75, 79
prayer flags, 83
preconceptions and expectations, 76
"primitive" cultures, 24, 27
    See also tribal/ethnic communities
Proust, Marcel, quote, 183
Pushkar, India, *xii*, 66–74

Q

Qaleraliq Glacier, 182

R

Raika, 70
Rajasthan, India, 29, 70, 73, 93
reading and literacy, 204–205
religious tourism. *See* sacred and religious sites
remote places
    impact of tourism, 183
    poverty in developing countries, 204–205
rental equipment for active/adventure tourism, 167
responsible tourism, 21–22
rhythm, as principle of design, 60
Rialto Bridge, 122, 125–127
Rift Valley, Kenya, *xi*, 17, 25, 146
rituals and ritualistic objects, 36, 75, 83
    rite of passage, 12–18
    river ceremony, 90, 94, 97
    See also sacred and religious sites
romantic ideas about modernity, 27
Roseau, Dominica, *xii*, 59
ruins, 113
rule of thirds, 5

S

sacred and religious sites, 75–106
    Buddhism, 80, 83, 85, 93, 101, 103, 178
    The Hall of Prayer for Good Harvests, China, 108
    Hinduism, 69–70, 88–97
    Id Kah Mosque, 35–36, 77
    Jerusalem, *ix*, 55, 86–87
    monks and monasteries, 80, 83, 100–101, 103–104, 178
    pilgrimages, 70, 75, 86–87, 97, 100, 103
    See also rituals and ritualistic objects
safari, 15, 17–18, 144–151
Saint Mark's Basilica, 129
Samburu, Kenya, 11, 140, 142, 146
Samburu Game Reserve, 14, 146
Samburu tribe, 12–20
San Bushmen, 194–201
San Juan, Puerto Rico, 57
sand and dust damage, 169
Santa Ana Cathedral, Mexico, 113
Santorini, Greece, 113
Sao Goncalo dos Campos, Brazil, 54
Sarnath, 93
saturation, 138
scale, 117, 136
scammers, hawkers, and beggars, *xiii*, 23–24, 65–66, 69, 73, 89, 93, 97
schools, education needs in poor countries, 204–205
"selfies," 4
Serengeti, 145–146
Serengeti-Mara, 144, 149
series of photographs, 110
shadows and highlights, 3, 78, 132–133, 136, 138
shadows inside buildings, 78
shape, as element of design, 57
sherpas, 177–179
Shiva, 88–97
"shot lists," 54
shutter speeds, 134, 136
shyness, 59, 65
sidelight, 7
silhouettes, 7, 85, 113, 117, 136, 138
silica packets to absorb condensation, 169
silk production, 40
simple scenes of everyday life, 55, 59, 61
snake charmer caste, 73
snapshots, understanding, 1–20
Songtsen Gampo, 101, 103
South Island, New Zealand, 135, 166
space, as element of design, 57
spectator point of view, 26
spiritual places. *See* sacred and religious sites
spot-meters, 136
stereotypes, 2, 30
storage and memory issues, 162
storms, 136–137
subsistence agriculture, 47–48
Sulamani Temple, Myanmar, 74
sunrises and sunsets, 136–137
survival skills, *xiii*
Swakopmund, Nambia, *xii*
synagogues. *See* sacred and religious sites

T

Taj Mahal, 115
Taklamakan Desert, 39–40, 169
Tangulbei, Kenya, 25
Tanzania, 145–146, 172
    Mount Kilimanjaro, 162
Taxkorgan, China, *xii*, 39
Tel Aviv, 55
Temple Mount, 86–87
temples. *See* sacred and religious sites
temporary nature of tourism, 204–205
texture, as element of design, 57
Thailand, *x*, 23, 26, 28–30, 61, 79, 81–82, 108, 111
thirds, rule of, 5
Thyangboche, Nepal, 76
Tibet, *viii*, 26, 58, 81, 98–105
Tjapukai, Australia, 24
Tokyo, 26
tone, as element of design, 57
tour guides, 32, 63, 101, 108, 141, 153, 161, 197
tourism industry, growth, 183
tourist traps, 2
tours specifically designed for photographers, 137
translators, 63
tratorria, 125–126
travel guides and brochures, 44, 54, 149–150
trekking in Nepal, 40–52
tribal/ethnic communities, 11–20, 30–31, 48, 70, 73, 194–201
    desert tribes, 27–28
    indigenous communities impact of tourism, 183
    indigenous people, 61
    Kikuyu, *xi*, 14
    Maasai people, 12–20
    Raika, 70
    remote places, impact of tourism, 183
    Samburu people, 12–20
    San Bushmen, 194–201
    Uyghur people, 35–36
tripods, 77, 79, 136
Turkey, 108
Turkistan, 36

U

underwater photography, 163, 165–167
UNESCO (United Nations Educational, Scientific, and Cultural Organization), 204–205
unity, as principle of design, 60
"us" and "them" effect, 22, 27
UV filters, 169

Uyghur people, 35–36

V

Valladolid, Mexico, 57
value, as element of design, 57
vanishing point, 166
Varanasi, India, 90, 93–94, 97
Venice, 122–129
vertical line, 114
viewpoint, 113
visual cues, 3
visual stimuli/human emotion connection, 6–7
visual weight, as principle of design, 60
volcanoes, 131, 143, 146, 184
voyeur point of view, 26, 114

W

warm and fuzzy feeling, 27
Wat Mahathat, Thailand, 82
Wat Yai Chai Mongkhon, Thailand, 108
water damage to equipment, 163, 165
weight, as principle of design, 60
Wellington, New Zealand, 140, 142
Western Wall, 86–87
White, Minor, quote, 75
white balance, 57
wide shots, 61
wildebeest, 144–146, 149–150
wildlife. *See* animals and wildlife
witness, point of view, 26
women, global literacy for, 205
workplaces, 59
World Education Forum, 205
worshipers. *See* sacred and religious sites

X

Xinjiang, China, 39, 42, 202, 204

Y

Yengi Bazaar, 36
Yucatan, Mexico, 167

Z

zebra, 149–150